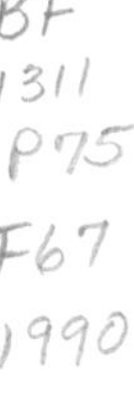

Table of Contents

Second of the Textbook Trilogy: *Truth for the New Age*

Letter to the Reader from the Brotherhood of God

The truth that we bring in "Masters of Greatness" is not surpassed by any other truth. Those who have worked with us before, and we expect that this number is legion by now, know how well our teamwork operates to bring life into alignment with all that is of God. You who approach us daily receive what is useful to you, no one else, and your lives reflect how much you have grown in spirit.

We know the innate worth of the books we have helped bring into their present form, for the material comes through the open channel from God-mind to the writer. She writes, with no reservations, exactly what God wants presented. We also work with her to answer her questions and to elucidate that which needs further explanation or examples. That which enters these books is not her own point of view.

With the teamwork of the writer, the God-mind itself and our stalwart help, the books come into being. We in this next plane of life who bring this message and who provide counseling team up with her being, her spirit, her reality. Then, spirit to spirit, we communicate to write these books.Those of you who read the first three books, **The Trilogy of Truth,*** know the details of this teamwork. Others may need to refer to those books for answers to their questions.

We call the truth in this book **prime truth.** It takes you past the point of "Eternal Gold"* into that which God-mind prepares to bring you safely into the New Age. Then you will point the way for others as well as help yourself.

Therefore, we must announce right now that this book is not for everyone! This book is for those who make the commitment to the New Age to help it evolve with good, with mercy and with the open truth in expression that will manifest the needs of those who seek survival. This book is for the new leadership, not the hangers-on, not those who do not want to survive into the New Age, not for those who want to believe us but still entertain doubts. This book is of ultimate value, so expensive in content that most will not buy it at the high cost we assess it to be.

Those who still remain with us to this point, however, will certainly team up with every intention of paying the cost, for they are already well into truth expression. Those readers are now invited to push forward in this book. It is not an easy book to understand, nor is it easy to use as a blueprint. But the rewards are great. Those who complete the reading of this book — and accept its message — will be masters of greatness, not servants of their fears or their doubts.

*__The Trilogy of Truth,__ by Jean K. Foster: *The God-Mind Connection,* 1987; *The Truth that Goes Unclaimed,* 1987; *Eternal Gold,* 1988.

Writer Discusses Her Assignment by Jean K. Foster

Intimidated by the goal of teaching the reader how to be a master of greatness, I doubted that I should be the one to write this book. After all, I was still trying to assimilate the truth of the first trilogy.* How could I expect to understand truth of the dimension the Brotherhood described?

A no nonsense communication from the Brotherhood of God changed my perspective, not an unusual occurrence in the months I have worked with this group of selfless spirits. "Humility," the Brotherhood said to me, "is not the tone to adopt here. Enter into bold acceptance of your destiny, not into insipid wavering over your worthiness or unworthiness."

Direct and to the point as always, the forthright Brotherhood cut through my denials and excuses. "Teamwork is in place, and we are ready to work with you," the message stated firmly. "Those who write this book through the writer know that it brings absolute truth that will enable the reader to be a master of greatness."

Therefore, I left my "insipid wavering" behind and moved into place at my keyboard with confidence in those who bring the truth through the open channel from God-mind . . . through my mind . . . and onto the manuscript.

*__The Trilogy of Truth,__ by Jean K. Foster: *The God-Mind Connection,* 1987; *The Truth that Goes Unclaimed,* 1987; *Eternal Gold,* 1988.

Showers of Blessings

1

What does it mean to be a master of greatness?

The Brotherhood began this book with the following words:

Oneness with God — the essential understanding of mankind — is written into the **Book of Truth** maintained by those who keep records of the great ones. Your name is there. Your perfect alliance with what is God is now read forth. Be alert. Be open. The words resound throughout this adjoining plane to join in the teamwork with those who will now help you be the true leaders of the New Age. To this end, the resounding words call forth your God potential.

Use this understanding well. Use this oneness with vigor, with awesome understanding, with the powerful means at your disposal. Those who eternalize well and put their truth on the line will give their best to those who follow them. They will be masters of greatness!

Many people will depend on these masters of greatness to give them their necessities. To give generously, to attend to the needs of others, to point the way toward the energy that will bring all that is right and good to those in need — that is how to see yourself using your God gifts. Those who turn to you for direction will turn as if to a father or mother. Those who depend on you for their bounty will depend on you as a child depends upon those who care for him. Those who team up with what is bright and good in the New Age will team up with you because you will know how to use the positive thrust of energy that gives life its perfection.

No one who is a master will have time for idleness, for the needs of people will be greater than there will seem to be hours in your day. But when you truly become a master of greatness, then you must give unstintingly of yourself for the good of others. That will be the result of becoming a master.

The writer wonders at the word "master." The kind of master we mean is not master over his fellows — no! The kind of master we tell of here is master over the great truth principles that will allow him to put truth to work in the world itself. Therefore, think not that you will have power to hurt others or to determine what people will do in any selfish way. Your mastery of principles only means that you now possess the power to give even as God gives. There is no mastery over the lives of others, only mastery over the principles that will point the way toward the good in life.

This book is organized into three parts. The first part concerns the tender truth in progress. "Tender" means new or unused. The next part covers truth without limit. The final thrust of the book pertains to the eternalization of truth into the greatness that becomes substance. "Greatness" refers to truth becoming one with earth material. Teaming up with each part, one at a time, will prevent confusion. Stay with the first part until you truly understand it. Then, and only then, go on with the second part. The third part, which we bring when you are ready, will nail down the procedure of becoming a master of greatness.

This chapter is only an opening of the book, remarks to get you into the right framework to receive the intended truth. Center yourself in your inner temple* where we will work with each one who intends to become a master. Center in the temple of your being where we will help you to understand all there is to understand in order to reach your goal. The inner temple will be our work place, our meeting place, our restitution to your mind of what was lost eons ago before spirits vacated the realm of God.

Blessings abound now, blessings of truth, blessings of growth. The Brotherhood rises as one to announce the culmination of our work through this writer in bringing this textbook in three parts, this series of three books that announce the New Age, teach those who grow into masters, and provide the guidebook that will organize the teamwork that will be needed as the earth goes into its travail.

Now, reader, if you still hold yourself ready to finalize your entity as a master of greatness, proceed into the next chapter where you will team up with the gentle presences who will teach you their own truth.

*See glossary

Your Learning Begins

2

How can I unlearn earth truth and grasp the God concepts of creativity?

Put away your preconceived notions of God. Put away your unhappy thoughts of the beginning of the New Age. Instead, hold out your mind to eternal truth — that wonderful God greatness that will turn your mind to opportunity, not devastation, to growth of goodness within the earth, not holocaust, to belief in creative human endeavors rather than vast agony and suffering.

Gently turn yourself toward the present revelation that comes now through this writer to give hope that God never deserts us. Not only does God never leave us, that which is God holds us up in strength and in understanding that we may unite with God truth to overcome all problems and all circumstances.

Thus the Brotherhood began the prologue to the course of study that leads one to the master's degree in perfect partnership with the God of the Universe.

You are now ready to take this adventurous trip with those in the Brotherhood who stand ready to assist you in becoming masters of greatness. Receive what we tell you without tearing each word, each thought into particles. That which needs explaining will be explained, and to fully enter in to this trip we take, you must give your mind/spirit its right to travel without permission. Lift your reservations and team up with adventure that will challenge your mind and bring you ideas you have never considered before.

We are sure you already understand the principles of putting God truth to work in the earth plane. No doubt you have read **The Trilogy of Truth*** and worked with the principles involved.

Once again we explain the meaning of "eternal truth." This God truth is stable and powerful as God is stable and powerful. This truth is unified principle that establishes universal partnership with the very nature of unlimited God. It will open your mind to the New Age and to the new circumstances in which you must live your life. This truth will also teach you an eternalization process that will give you a new perspective on planet earth. That which is our true partnership with God and with you will be discussed in this chapter to enable you to become the person who can lead others.

Do not repeat what we tell you as if the mere repeating of it will bring you power. That earthbound attitude toward truth will not do. Instead, open your mind to the farthest reach of the universe. There, so far that you have never even heard of it, sits the star we wish you to contemplate. Put yourself into the range of this star's glow, its purity. Bring it into your being as you would bring pure light, pure glory. Your being rises in tone, rises in energy, for this star is even now receiving creative pulses.

The star's whirling energy generates positive ions of power which stir the atmosphere around it. You stand in the midst of this powerful statement of what God IS, knowing that what you see is real. To understand truth, you must enter into the picture we put before you, for to accept this star's existence without proof is what you must be ready to enter into your being.

The obviousness of what we say may strike some of you as elementary. You may feel like we talk to you as to a child. But never think of any God truth as elementary. The truth of what we tell you may appear like basic understanding of spiritual things, and you may, therefore, overlook its vast importance. To be a master of greatness, you must not resist the teaching; you must not think you are too advanced to learn anything new.

The success or the failure of this enterprise depends upon your attitude.Therefore, examine your reaction to our words about the existence of an unseen star. Team up with what we say here. Can you release your preconceived notions of what is known and what is to be learned? Begin once again as a child would begin. Turn your face trustingly to the face of truth.

Now, work with this attitude until it is truly yours. No self-righteousness will help you to become a master. No attitude of superiority will team up with any of the advanced truth that will plummet you into your graduate study of truth. The attitude you must evidence here is one of giving your open mind, your quiet reflection, your trust in the truth, your own spirit that is now ready for the growth that must come with this study.

The principle we must now lay before you, if you are indeed ready with the new, enlightened attitude and the burning commitment, is this: **The world is not remotely what most people think it is. The world is the tender presence that opens itself to perfection.** The world that you know and believe in is not matter alone. The world manifests matter because spirit tells it to manifest. The earth is the essence of what its spirit self, its tender presence which handles the eternalizations of growth, wants manifested.

To understand this principle, you must view the earth as the manifestation, not as matter. When you get this viewpoint instated within your own being, you can work with the planet that responds to its own entity, that tender presence from God that is responsible for keeping earth what it must be in order to maintain life.

Yes, maintaining life on planet earth is very important to the entire universe. This planet is here to provide the opportunity that our spirit selves need to bring their truth into realization. Therefore, bringing this planet into its present state where it supports life is supreme creativity. This creativity works constantly. It is never inactive. The entering truth declares that this planet is the best in the universe for entering into life forms in which the spirit self can then advance.

Those who enter into life forms want the earth to continue. They devote themselves entirely, when they understand how vital it is, to the task of being part of the creative process that contributes to the good. Therefore, you who now want to be masters of greatness must be open to this understanding. Those who intend to take leadership in the New Age must understand the reasons why this planet is important and why the operating principles of creativity must be held as sacred and inviolate.

The principle we have given you is the basis of this understanding. To omit this principle is to make the obvious mistake of calling the earth "matter," and not "God substance." Be into the understanding presented here. Those who declare that the planet is "matter" open themselves only to earth-mind truth which reports what it sees physically. Those who perceive beyond the obvious will see that this planet is composed of God substance because it is governed by the spirit of creativity, the entity which is tenderly working with the planet.

Those who may be reading this book without prior understanding will never comprehend what is made plain here. Those who have oriented their thinking to the spiritual base will know exactly what is meant.

Give time to this principle; do not move hastily past this point. But when you have sufficient understanding, read on.

The next principle we will discuss is the principle of greatness. To understand it, you must meditate quietly until your inner being unites with the principle. **That**

which is greatness responds only to God-mind. The greatness that we speak of here is God-mind working through individual minds. Therefore, the principle works like this: to master the greatness that God gives you, become totally open to becoming one with the teamwork of God and the tender presences.**

Think on this principle and its explanation phrase by phrase. Team up with the idea piece by piece. Give its impact to your spirit self. Then, when you believe you are ready, hold out the principle to catch its thrust. The thrust we speak of is the marvelous energy that pours forth through your own being when this principle is put into motion. The motion is caused when you work with the principle, when you bury it within your being, when you open to the idea of its usefulness.

Now that you have read, studied, held the two principles to your innermost self, you can consider how these principles will affect the world you live in. Team up. Team up. Team up!

The world you operate within is not static. Its being quivers with creative energy. That being which is the open truth of the planet is the teammate you must turn your attention to, not the matter that rises and falls, the matter that rends itself open or belches forth its earth energy. No, your attention must go to the working principle within, the creative spirit, the being who wants only the good of the planet to be evidenced.

Then you can work with the two principles we have given in this chapter, for you now understand how they tie the teamwork together, how they will operate within the universe, how they will bring into motion that which you will need to live in greatness.

If you do not understand what we say, go back and review the principles. The one says that the God of the Universe is the Teammate with whom you want to unite. This principle is basic to proper understanding of manifesting greatness. The second deals with the perspective of the planet, world or earth you live on. This planet is not out there in the universe without plan, without good enterprising action. The planet has a base of potential greatness because the very earth responds to the spirit that offers creativity.

Now, do you understand? If not, review it all from the beginning of the chapter. When, and only when, you feel ready, read further.

The wind and the rain respond to the creative spirit because they must. They know not what turn to take nor what operating plan to follow. They wait for the command.

Then why, I wondered to myself, does the planet experience droughts and floods? My thoughts were heard as if I had shouted, and the Brotherhood answered.

The overworked planet is not understood by those who inhabit it. They work on their own goals, oblivious of the goals of the planet. Therefore, people turn to the planet as to a "thing" and not as to a spirit. They think, "Take what I want. This earth replenishes itself, and I must have these trees, this land, this great expanse of earth for my own purposes." They never turn to the earth to learn the creative plan, to learn how the eternal truth holds the planet in its understanding. Therefore, the great plan is turned on its head by those who have never understood the reality of the earth.

Those who address themselves to the creativity, those who hold the understanding within them that the earth is not a 'thing,' not a vast place that is there for their use, will team up with the creative spirit that holds the planet as spirit first, matter second. The way such people address the earth unites the purpose with the being of creativity, and the earth and the people prosper.

I interrupted to ask, "By 'address the earth,' do you mean literally? Are we to talk to the earth — send out questions about how to farm our crops, how to wisely use the forests, how to conserve water?"

We use "address the earth" to point out that earth is governed by spirit, not the whim of mankind. Though the earth seems to respond to the whim of man, in truth it does not. People may take what they want, and they may team up with materiality; but the earth must respond to its inner self, the spirit that proclaims that it is truth in expression.

Still puzzled, I asked, "If people can use the earth's bounty for their own materialistic purposes, then how do we know that the earth must respond to its spirit?"

By the way the earth now groans with its eternalizations of helplessness in the face of people's great misunderstanding. By the entering of this New Age that will bring much turmoil to mankind but much hope for renewal to the planet. By these signs you will know the truth.

I asked if it is too late to "address the earth" and turn things around.

The signs are in place already. The turn-around you want is within the New Age, not within the hope of mankind to forestall their involvement in the new eternalizations that will move the planet into a new polarity.

Better truth (that earth is not a thing) is not possible, for at the root of many problems in life is the misunderstanding that the earth is matter to be treated as matter by those who need its wealth. Bringing new open truth into being within the earth is the point of the New Age. This newness is needed to open the earth to its potential, to its creativity in motion.

No person on the face of the planet will go along without recognition of the New Age, and people will be dismayed because they will not know why the changes come about. Those who become masters of greatness, however, will lead others into the places where they may not only survive, but where they may live life under new orders. The new orders are those which now open to you, the reader. These orders respond to God-mind truth, they will lead with kindness and understanding, and they will even bring you whatever it is you will need and want in the new life to come.

This, then, is the prologue that you, the reader, must take into your thoughts, take into your center, your pure spirit self. Those who want to make themselves the masters of truth must, now that the prologue is understood, ready themselves to be open to the ever challenging truth that pours through this writer and onto the machine which will print it. Those who enter into each understanding will know the opening greatness that is bound to obey the bright truth of the universe.

No one who opens to our truth will be disappointed. Nor will the student of greatness, if he is teamed up with the Brotherhood, eternalize what is not perfect expression. You, therefore, are now putting your feet onto the pathway to God-mind, the pathway to eternal and personal truth, the pathway that leads to perfect manifestation of truth in the world about you.

Become eternalizers of truth, eternalizers of what the truth allows you to do. Never hold back. Never crawl on your knees in hesitancy and in humility and in the fear of God. No, we say! The one who is with the God of the Universe, the one who recognizes his own identity through his oneness with God, that one will manifest truth with greatness instilled within him or within her. The God of the Universe reaches forth to express greatness to the earth that is now undergoing its eternalization of purity. God reaches forth in the men and women who inhabit this earth and who want to applaud the New Age as what the earth needs. They do not hesitate or condemn God, nor do they find fault with others who have lived before them. They hold out no need to identify the ones responsible. They go on with the work of greatness — the work that God does with their own teamwork. That's the way greatness works.

Every man, woman and child will be affected by the change in the earth. The seasons will change because the earth moves to a new polarity. The winds will increase, and there will be a time when many fear the end of the planet itself. But you who know truth will never embrace the thought of destruction, for you know the New Age heralds the good to come. You, instead, turn within to your truth center to recognize the spirit at work in this entire situation. As you open yourself to our help and as you turn within to the open channel of truth that comes through you from God-mind Itself, you will begin to build the true world of thought where truth and God meet.

You will oppose those who decry the God they think brought the holocaust. You will oppose those who team up to survive but who care nothing for others. They will receive exactly what they expect to find. You who become masters of greatness, however, will give your truth to others and help to put truth in motion for everyone. The opposing forces will team up against you, but you will be able to defend yourself and others around you. No, there will be no armaments needed. No, there will be no help in the way of soldiers. There will be, however, the manifestation of truth which proclaims that you who are the teammate of God can be invincible.

Truth that enters to be proved in the earth plane is now being stored up within you. The truth is eternal and it is personal, and you stand within its protective teamwork. Therefore, hold yourself ready to team up with us when the New Age comes that you may quickly enact the truth to benefit mankind and to usher in the age of peace and God truth.

Now open your heart to us, open your gentleness, your tenderness. You will be the one who now decides that you can be a master, and you will be able to go forward in this book to receive the lessons that will proclaim your mastery over these principles. Give us your truth center, your being that opens itself to bloom in mighty triumph over earth-mind thought. Nothing that enters now can ever give you harm, for we are there with you to help you become one with the **pure truth,** the **pure thought,** the **pure light** that shines on you through God-mind.

The truth that enters this chapter is now ready to be absorbed to prepare the reader to accept the mighty words that are to come. Therefore, do not hasten to read further, candidate for greatness, but study, refine your being, your truth center, your spirit self, that you will more easily team up with what is to come.

*__The Trilogy of Truth,__ by Jean K. Foster: *The God-Mind Connection,* 1987; *The Truth that Goes Unclaimed,* 1987; *Eternal Gold,* 1988.

**See glossary

The Brotherhood of God and You

3

What kind of teamwork will help me to manifest God truth as material substance?

As this chapter began, I knew I was way over my head. There was no time allotted me for refining my being and absorbing the ideas presented in the last chapter. Because of the urgency of writing this book, I was asked to persevere.

Bring your Pure Truth into the open that we may help you to put it into evidence within the earth plane. This is our call to you who will be the masters — the leaders, the wayshowers of the New Age — to gently step forth to become the truth in motion.

Truth in motion is, of course, the positive thrust of God energy teaming up within you to put the satisfying truth right there in the world you live in. Ready yourself to open your mind further than you have ever opened it before. To become a master of truth, you must hold no reservations about practicing its principles and its laws. To withhold your gentle self from involvement is tantamount to giving us an eternalization (firm picture or idea) of cooperation, but then withdrawing it as too personal, too great a risk to take.

No one who understands what we say will want to give us a sign of cooperation and then give us another signal that you have withdrawn because the task is too demanding, or that the task requires too much of your personal privacy. No one who wants greatness would turn away. The eternal truth and your personal truth are there to enjoy. The opportunity is here — the opportunity you have long awaited. The Brotherhood teams up with you to put you in touch with the highest possible expression of the truth that you have accepted for yourself.

Teamwork is the key to insight and understanding. It makes possible an eternal alliance that will bring you to the point of expressing God truth in the living of your life. The Brotherhood will help you to hurdle doubts, inappropriate expectations, selfish thoughts and eternalizations of unimportant things. We will elevate your thoughts so you may eternalize God truth that will develop into great good not only for you, but for others, too. In this way we can enter into your gentle presence to help you to develop the understanding that a master must have.

A master needs to put truth into the eternalization each time he teams up with us. The eternalization must reflect the great good which the God of the Universe presents to your mind. Not all masters will have the same assignments. Truth that comes to some will not come to others. What each person receives depends on his assignment. These eternalizations that team up with God truth will begin the process, and they are the truth that you hold in mind as the entering goodness or material expression of truth.

Now that you have this initial understanding, let us use an example. A person who has decided to be a master knows he has a special interest in the truth that will help people in some particular way. Perhaps your speciality is bringing shelter into form. **The entering good will be the actual shelter that people can use to house themselves.** The truth back of this entering goodness, however, is not "shelter is good;" it is the teamwork that you enter into with the Brotherhood and the God of the Universe. **This teamwork connects**

your idea of need with the Brotherhood who know that each need can be met when the thought is teamed up with the right energy. With this structure in mind, you and the Brotherhood unite to bring a clarity of thinking to the plan. What kind of shelter is needed? How big? How many? What kind?

This eternalization is developed clearly between us, and then we both take this eternalization to the God of the Universe — that Source of all Good. Teaming up with the Source — and we in the Brotherhood help you to accomplish this — the shelter arrives through the ether to become one with the God substance from which all things are made. The shelters, therefore, arrive where they are needed. That is the way it works — no sweat of the brow, no complicated construction manual!

The writer says, "Wow! This kind of construction is hard to bring about." This wetting (diluting) of the truth is her own energy that runs downhill and away to no result! This message must be brought into understanding not by wonderment, not by opinions on how such a thing can happen! No!

Thinking that what we describe is a miracle only reflects earth-mind thought. But if you focus on teamwork, understanding will grow within you, the understanding of how to use God truth in creative endeavors.

The eternalizations that you hold — both positive and negative — work in the outer world. Therefore, when you say, "Wow!" and stand back in wonderment, you enter into a negative thrust, a limiting concept. What happens then? You offset the positive thrust, and the energy just twinges a bit and recedes into that from which it came.

Needs that arise in the New Age must be met by the process of teaming up with the Brotherhood, or they may not be met in time to help those who are without homes, food and clothing. **Wonderment must not enter into better understanding.** What is needed is acceptance of what we bring you in the way of furthering your skill at putting truth into expression.

Now then, tune your spirits into the open channel that, by now, you have learned to make on your own. Tune in to this channel to learn what your area of responsibility will be in the New Age. What is your assignment? What will you work with when the New Age comes? What must you now practice? We need your cooperation here. Practice will help you work with greater authority when the new polarity is given by the God whose creativity is even now at work. Your assignment is noted. We who work with records have written down your name and your assignment. Then, when the time comes, we will know how to work with each master.

Since the Brotherhood insisted that the writer participate in all things, I paused to learn my own assignment.

That which you do now is what you will do then — put forth the truth that will help people become their potential. In this way you will serve others and your own needs too. The giving of truth will be your speciality.

The Brotherhood continued.

Get into the realm of spirit to work wonders. The spirit will be in charge in the New Age, for earth truth will no longer hold true. That which has accumulated throughout the ages will be wiped out, and you will be among those who will instate new God truth in its place. Understand that the earth will receive **only** God truth, none other. Various thoughts of fear or hate or great agitation will not affect earth in its turmoil over growing into greater good. The earth will respond only to those truths that generate more good for the planet. Therefore, to meet the conditions as you find them, you must work with your spirit self.

Putting greater good into the earth will be your work — yours and those other masters who will be prepared to overcome earth truth with God truth. Your assignment will be whatever your spirit self claims as its own particular interest, its own speciality. No one master will have the entire process at hand; the entire process takes the teamwork of many. That is the way it will be in the New Age when we who work with the earth and those who survive take the eternal truth into the earth plane.

Be eternally vigilant to attain the highest expression of truth. Be constantly prepared to hold no assignment too hard or too great a task. Your limited thought, your reticence or your back turned to the task at hand will eliminate any idea of greatness teaming up within you. Your thought may stray, but never entertain that stray thought that offers no good to you or to anybody else. Throw it out even as it appears to you. Turn to the Brotherhood to get help, for their fortuitous claim is to be that help when you need it.

Be tuned to greatness, to your potential, to that which wants to flow through you into the world. Then you will be righteousness itself, the God self expressing, the truth in expression. Tune to the being within, that great I Am that God claims as one with Him, one with His goodness, His power, His opportunities that will be given fulfillment.

Getting the Most for Your Perfect Truth

4

How can I release my awe and fear of the New Age and align myself with all that God IS?

The perfect truth for you, a candidate for a master of greatness, is what you receive directly through God-mind. You have already entered into the open channel to that Source, that Perfection, that Goodness. Therefore, you have experienced the wonderful truth that pours out to renew your spirit and to help you to live in the earth plane.

However, to wrest full value from that truth, you must team up with what we tell you in this chapter. No previous understanding on the matter of getting full value has been given the writer of these books. Therefore, unless you have, on your own, worked through this challenge, you have not read what we now present.

When I began writing with the Brotherhood, I thought we would do well to put one book together. As that book drew to a conclusion, I truly believed that it contained everything that could be said in the way of truth. Therefore, it was with considerable surprise that I learned that "The God-Mind Connection" was the first book in a trilogy. Soon the second book, "The Truth that Goes Unclaimed," was outlined, and* *we were involved in Chapter 1. As the second book closed, the Brotherhood outlined the third book, "Eternal Gold." The advanced spirits in the Brotherhood continue to surprise me, but not with the fact of a second trilogy. The surprise comes from the truth itself — its depth, its logic, its consistency, its challenge to me and to the reader. Just when I think I am as full of truth as I can possibly be, those messengers from the Brotherhood bring even greater truth from God-mind.*

I had hoped, as I said in Chapter 2, to be the one who conveys this truth to you, not to be a candidate myself. But the Brotherhood insists that I will be a better writer if I do all that the reader does to master the truth that is brought to you in this book. Also, I am told that my growth plan includes not only writing these books but becoming one with as much truth as possible here in the earth plane. Therefore, when I ask questions, I ask as a student. The questions will reflect my own concerns, but I hope they will be helpful to all who read these words.

The message from the Brotherhood continued.

Now it is time to open fully and without hesitation to that which we call "teamwork." We have talked "teamwork" again and again, right? We have said, "Team up!" many, many times. You, in your eagerness, have probably opened your mind to this suggestion when we have presented it before. But now we enter into a new thought on the subject. Ready yourself to play a game of leaping through the teamwork to receive the desired object that you want entered into your world. Yes, we said "a game" because we want you to relax and enter into what we suggest with eager enthusiasm, with a spirit of great adventure.

Ready? Prepare yourself by stretching your body muscles and at the same time stretch your mind muscles. Open your being to the farthest spot in the Universe that you can imagine and then stand there! Will you be afraid away out there? Eternalize your being in space standing on a planet that has teeming life force. That force is not fearsome. It is the universal God working within that planet to bring it into perfection.

The seas stir and steam. The sky has red hues and mists that deepen around you. The eternal truth is all you know right now, for there is nothing else to rely on way out there in a planet as yet unfinished, as yet uninhabited by the beings you are used to. In fact, you see no sign of growth, no sign of life forms. There is only the rolling, the stirring, the heaving of earth and seas. You stand securely, however, and you fear nothing.

Why don't you fear? Because the truth is instated within you that God is the Being Who governs the entire creative spirit of the universe. Why fear? God has nothing fearful to bring into manifestation. You want nothing fearful, do you? You want no pointless struggle with the forces you perceive in motion, for you know these forces to be God. Therefore, you do not resist your surroundings or try to escape. You stabilize, in fact. Yes, you become the certain being, the sure spirit, the credulous soul who stands in the midst of a heaving planet and knows there is nothing to fear.

The truth washes over you that this planet is God's creative work, and you hold your being in its rhythm. Within yourself you find the same rhythm that is present in the undulating planet. As you bring your gentle being into this rhythm, you understand God at work.

Yes, God at work. The mists rise easily, sweetly, not in anger or in harsh expression. The waves of the sea swing one way and then another because they must respond to the spirit within the planet which, in turn, responds to the God of the Universe. Then you, in your wisdom, your personal and perfect truth, respond to this same rhythm. The creative energy rises within you, for God's rhythm initiates your own creative impulses. Then you sway with the waves, rise with the mists, team up with the matter which begins to form within the planet.

Nothing that enters you is wrong, nor is it against nature. It is nature at its best, for it is nature in response to the God of the Universe. This greatness stirs your own being, and you respond to it with utter understanding. The truth opens to you in full, and you team up with all you have learned while standing on this planet in the far reaches of the universe.

What have you absorbed in this experience? Think. Hold the experience within you again. Believe it. What have you learned?

You have learned how to persevere when the outer presence is unlike anything you have ever known. Yes, you stood fast, and you were unafraid. You learned to ride the waves of creativity knowing that God is indeed in charge of this activity. You were not afraid; you were able to look about you and know that what you saw was God at work. There was nothing in that experience to make you afraid. That's what you learned.

Now you are ready to face another entering truth that will help you to develop your potential and to express truth to the utmost. Enter into our own counsel through your inner temple.** Wait to know what to do next. What is your temple at this point?

What shall your temple bring into your life? Enter the temple and wait for us. We come with laughter because we feel wonderful about working with you. You receive us wreathed in smiles. We sit down together near a fountain, if you have one, or near a pond, if you put one in, or we sit upon new embroidered cushions, or we float in the temple with you, neither standing nor sitting, just being there in the glow of your temple.

Now watch what we do within your temple! We sweep it away! We fold it up to put it away, and we still float with you in the space where you had a temple. But there is no comforting temple. The temple has been taken away, not to be replaced with a new temple, but to give you a sense of being in space without the beauty you put within your temple. There is nothing here, nothing of beauty. We who float with you wait to see what you will do. We team up with you, hold your hands if you wish, stay near you while you get over the shock of not having a temple. Then we wave farewell and vanish. You send us thoughts to come back, but we do not. You are there alone.

What do you notice now? What is beginning to enter your mind? To rebuild? Perhaps. To resign yourself to aloneness? Perhaps. To hear the inner beat of creativity, or to hear the heartbeat of spirit? You begin to hear it while you float in the darkness — the beat that is entirely God's, no other! Only God's heartbeat could be what you hear, for there is no other presence near. You respond to this beating, to this force that grows stronger as you grow more aware. As you center on this beat, you know that nothing else matters — not the temple, not the Brothers who came to stand by you, not the physical earth which is material. Only this beating, this call that God gives to his own co- creators.

What have you learned here? What is yours to keep? What message penetrates your being?

That heartbeat is your God-mind connection beating loudly and clearly. It is your link to What Is — entering truth, great understanding, great knowledge — to the beginning of all that is God truth in expression. Do you understand our message? Do you see the thing we teach you here?

The outpouring of truth stopped, and I pursued this experience — my awareness of the heartbeat of God. Could I, would I, hear and/or feel this heartbeat? The Brotherhood, not waiting for my ultimate experience to occur, resolutely continued.

Now then, hold yourself ready to further your understanding. We who operate truth channeling to help those who cannot help themselves know that there is great strength entering those of you who have persevered through this series of books. We know that you open yourselves to greatness even now. Therefore, hold no thought of withholding your own worth. Team up with us as equals, not as learners, not as beginning students. You who study with us are now bringing challenges to your candidacy and beginning your teamwork tests.

We will now take one student apiece — one teacher, one student. In that way, you will go faster in your work and develop your potential more speedily than you would by the group method. We will explain how you will work. We who enter to work with you will team up with those we best help. Those whose tones match most perfectly will work together. This matching is done to keep us compatible, to keep us happily in tune.

The operating schedule we will have depends on your availability to work with your teacher. The time must be set. The hour must be noted. The time is important — not to the teacher who will enter whenever you say, but to you, the candidate who wants to put his mastery of greatness on the line.

Our teamwork will begin with recognition of you and your teacher who is here with the right tone. You who want to be a master must hold the door of your being open to the idea of association before the teacher can enter therein. To work with a teacher on this side, to reap great value from one-on-one teaching and learning, you must open your mind to the entering truth. We who will be teachers hold ourselves in readiness to team up with you.

Now let us review momentarily to be sure we know that each entering truth has been stated properly. First, there is an understanding that you, the candidate, will present your being before the Brotherhood to be taught. Right? Then, having met the tests we proposed, you open yourself to a teacher who is the exact one you need. Then you are ready to learn.

Be true to your own being in this work, and hold yourself open to receiving new truth. Be one who understands the goal — that of being a master of greatness. Then you will not stray from the entering truth that will put you in the seat of powerful management of the eternal truth as well as your personal truth. Keep strong, both in spirit and in body. Put your truth to work in your body to be able to express that which the spirit brings forth. Neglect your own body, and you neglect the vehicle needed to help those who go into the New Age. The body is your responsibility, your concern, yours to care for and to govern.

Team up with each and every personal truth because these truths will be the building blocks which express in the earth plane. Yes, the truth becomes substance because it must, not because of any magic that will happen. Never depend on magic, candidate! Hold only to truth that enters you to be expressed!

Be gentle with yourself, not harsh. Tenderly urge yourself forward, not giving in to self berating or self flagellation. Why punish the body that is the house that you live in? The body only responds to the spirit, not vice versa. Therefore, get the understanding straight in your mind that you, the creative God self within you, is the one in charge, not the body self.

Our teaching method will be outlined in the chapters to come. In this way we have a text or study guide from which we can proceed. The teacher will work with you at whatever pace is needed, and you will team up with this teacher to learn the material in whatever way seems best for you. Hold an open mind and an open heart toward this study. Perhaps none of you has ever studied in quite this way. But whether or not you perfectly understand how it will work, you must know now and with certainty that the God of the Universe is at the heart of this study. The words reflect the great truth of the Universal I Am.

Now tell the calm quiet spirit within you to begin the study. Set the time and hold to it. If there must be some change, then notify the teacher as you would an earthly teacher. This is not because the teacher will not know, but because if you will work in tandem, you must honor appointments as you would honor those made within your earth plane.

The next chapter teaches a fundamental truth, one you must hold within you as basic. Therefore, call forth your teacher and say you are ready to begin.

We salute you, candidate! We salute your energy, your decision to become a master, and we bring you our best help — the worthy energy that now operates in and around you. Whenever you feel weakened in any way, call for this energy, and we who work with energy will bring it to you. In this way, you will keep the dedication, the health, the enthusiasm that is needed in this work.

* **The Trilogy of Truth,** by Jean K. Foster; *The God-Mind Connection*, 1987; *The Truth that Goes Unclaimed*, 1987; *Eternal Gold*, 1988.

** See glossary

Becoming the Truth in Expression

5

Why must my understanding of gravity and the earth's orbit of the sun change?

Following the directions of the Brotherhood on how the truth would be taught, I asked for a personal teacher. By way of the open channel, an advanced spirit came who began by measuring my energy level.

"I am recording this in my record," the advanced spirit who was to be my teacher said. "I need your energy level to give me an idea of how to team up with you."

To help me understand our relationship, my teacher gave further explanation.

"You now have a personal eternalization of a teacher, and this is the one whom you will find working within your temple to help you to assimilate the truth in the book you now write. Your picture is vague, I see. But eternalizations are often cloudy when the entity doesn't know what to expect."

My teacher was absolutely right. My mental picture was anything but clear. In fact, the image I held in mind was almost vaporous. Building a true eternalization with the help of my teacher would not be possible until I became a true teammate. Further instruction came.

"Put your own resistance aside and be open with me."

And I, as yet unwilling to do as my teacher suggested, asked, instead, for his name.

"Team up! Team up with the one who enters to help you to learn, the one who opens himself to your truth center in the matter of helping you be a master of greatness. Yes, I am a master of greatness. The teachers are all masters of greatness who enter to help those in the earth plane who want to be masters too. Call me the tender teammate, the one who gives you help."

I persisted. "No personal name?" I asked, and back came the answer.

"No personal name, Truth-giver. I am Teacher; you are Truth-giver."

The name "Truth-giver" was given me long ago when the first truth book was being written. Apparently what we are is vastly more important than who we are. I stopped the questions and said that we would meet most days in the morning around 9 a.m., and I promised to let my teacher know when the schedule must be changed. I asked if this plan was satisfactory, and my teacher replied.

"The time is now entered into my record. The truth will be presented, and we will work together, you and I, to wrest from it its value in your life."

Our experiences — me as the writer and you as the reader —will be different. When you tune into the open channel, you will be met by a teacher who is best suited to you. I only tell you my experience to assure you that the teamwork is in place and working.

Following the dialogue with my teacher, the Brotherhood now began a chapter that will stretch your mind farther than it has ever been stretched. The helper or teacher who manifested to you and me will most assuredly be there to help us assimilate this truth.

You who enter into this graduate study to be masters of greatness can enjoy our work better if you will eternalize as we will teach you now. Give us your teamwork, your open minds, your fearless attitudes that stand ready to enter into the adventurous wisdom that we bring into this textbook.

Never before, perhaps, have you read such an invitation in a textbook. The reason we approach you in this manner is that we know what results you may expect. The subject matter you study here is not for those who view the world with the attitude of unbelievers. The subject matter you find here is for those who now abandon that which their minds have previously held as inviolate earth truth. Yes, though you have advanced to this point, there must be certain things that you still hold inviolate. Right? What are these truths? What are these inviolate truths that you think in your inner self cannot be omitted from your mind/soul?

One may be the power of gravity. The entity who first named the power and explained it was only reflecting the order of things as he saw them. He gave names to what he saw that others might deal with that law. You who stand here in readiness to be masters have long accepted the law of gravity as inviolate, right? To turn away from this law will cause consternation, perhaps, but we now eternalize before you the way things really are in the earth plane.

The law that is named "gravity" is not the law that masters will need in their work. The law is only manmade, not a law that God-mind created. Being caught up in gravity holds you into the materialism that is earth, not the creative spirit which is also earth. Therefore, hold no truth that comes from the past as a law at all. Instead, turn to spirit for better truth.

Now we will advance your understanding that you may supplant the old law with a new and better law that enters through God-mind. The law we now give is called **The Law of Teamwork.** This spiritual law notes that you are the one who, with the teamwork of the God of the Universe, will bring new truth to earth, new expressions into being, new teamwork into the vast ignorance of those who inhabit the planet.

Yes, **The Law of Teamwork** circumvents any and all laws that earth-mind projects, no matter how enlightened that earth-mind law may seem. The spiritual law is way above any and all earth-mind laws. Do you have that understanding in your mind? Do you understand what is said? Is the law within you fully? Then you may proceed with your teacher's help.

At this point the teachers may want to quiz you, the candidate, on your understanding. Accept the entire thrust of their help; hold nothing back; hold onto no truth that needs overturning.

I turned to my teacher who told me that the "wresting of the truth was open to me." By this statement the master of greatness meant that I knew the lesson of **The Law of Teamwork** *(God-mind truth) as opposed to* **the law of gravity** *(earth-mind truth). I expressed the truth as I understand it, and my teacher said, "The truth is yours." The Brotherhood continued.*

Never team up with other earth entities in this study. They must work individually even as you work individually. The teachers who work with you will be your companions on the pathway, and this companionship will sustain you in this work within your being. This way you will know how to work fully with one on the next plane, one who will help you in the days ahead, into the New Age which you must confront.

The overturning of the primary law of gravity having been accomplished, you are ready to rescind yet another law. This one holds that earth responds in orbit to the sun. You, who learned this truth in school, will have difficulty abandoning this idea because you seem to have known it all your life. Yet the sun is only in the universe because the truth of God opens to this partnership between earth and sun. Yes, the sun is not the stable thing in the universe that you perceive it to be. The sun is able to respond to its own spiritual understanding, its own creative spirit. Therefore, relating to the sun that appears to rise in the east and set in the west is only the earth-mind explanation of a spiritual truth — that the sun is the focus of truth as the earth is the focus of truth.

You see, the two spirits are one with God, one with the creative universe. The ones who work in the midst of creative spirit must view the universe with "new eyes" or "new understanding." The sun, that ball of fire, that immense source of light and heat, that most needed entity that you view out there is not calling earth to it. Be open to this understanding. The sun moves and has its being within the immense creative spirit of the God of the Universe. The spirit earth has its center in this same God. Therefore, the reason we give you that the earth circles the sun in its orbit is that the God of the Universe holds the two in position, in eternal truth, in the energetic crisscross of tonal melody. The orbit is in syncopation with the rhythm of Creative Spirit, with the God of the Universe.

No other law that earth-mind puts forth can stand against this understanding which is yours, and which you may learn to work with. The one who works with you will hold you in this Light of God, this partnership with what is of God. You, a candidate for master of greatness, are now opening to the wisdom that God-mind pours forth for your understanding and acceptance. When you master these principles, you will then learn how to make use of your knowledge.

The obvious answer is only superficial. Team up with the God that you know through the open channel and go to Him for insight.

By following this advice, I heard the wisdom behind the sun and the earth that turns to God, even as my spirit turns to God. My teacher told me to "enter into the wisdom with open mind and open heart" that I may understand it with my entire being.

Take the two laws we have presented and work with them in your mind according to what your teacher suggests. There may be some who want to "prove" these laws in one way or another. Others may fall away, for now, wrestling with reason and the intellectual self that proclaims facts given in earth as facts that even God must accept.

But whatever holds you back, rest assured that the hesitation and turning away you feel are only temporary. You are, after all, beings who have eternal truth within you, who have personal truth instated also. You must now perform this truth.

To enter into the eternalization that will require your mastery of those laws which we have laid before you, you must turn only to God-mind, not to earth- mind. There are, perhaps, some of you who thought you had turned from earth-mind thought, and those of you who now hesitate wonder how you can totally abandon truths which seem so obvious to anyone.

Therefore, we urge you who have these thoughts to get your basic understanding well in mind. Turn back to the previous chapter and review it. Turn to your constant companion and teacher who will give you guidance in this matter. Go to your God-mind connection and ask, "What about this book that says I am to abandon my belief in the law of gravity and the law that says the earth orbits the sun. What is this truth that projects itself to me?" The truth of God will then pour through to you, and you will know with certainty that this textbook is not questioning God, it questions only the material concepts.

Be eternally reasonable with your demands on yourself. Do not worry if you hold back. The part that resists must be dealt with piece by piece. The opinions that earth-mind has dealt out through your lifetime on earth and before are imbedded in the fabric of your environment. That is why it is hard to undo your acceptance of what seems most reasonable. That is why you work with each word to wrest from it the truth of God that can supplant any and all lesser truth. You will win this grade — the grade of "A" for "Acceptance."

Be clear in what you think. Murky thoughts produce murky results. If you question why gravity is the lesser truth, think through both truths and hold them out to God-mind. But if you simply steam the window of your mind due to our explanation of the truth of God being the only truth that is worth paying attention to, then you will receive no clear answer.

We want you to receive new truth and to open to new concepts about these two laws. They are now ready to be put where they deserve to be — in the history books of the planet. They deserve a place there because they show how people turned to material explanations and thus derived earth satisfaction in the explanations. But what people lost was of infinitely more value, for they lost the heart of truth — that man working with God may team up to produce great creative thought in the outer environment. No gravity, no orbiting will erase the truth. They only cloud the matter and prevent man from opening himself to God to accomplish greatness.

About now you may wonder how greatness will be done. But soon enough you will begin working with these new concepts to bring greatness into your own environment. We who bring this textbook to the writer call upon you to study, get ready, and eventually we will move into the open where mankind may witness the greatness in operation.

Meanwhile, work with these spiritual principles until they are one with you. Observe gravity at work; think on the concept we present that will supplant that law. Then you will be prepared to work with your environment. The same goes for the earth orbiting around the sun. The greatness that is inherent within the understanding of earth and sun as two spirits which respond to God truth will be the key to working with your planet to bring greatness into being.

The writer holds that which is written here as tremendous in concept, and she believes that it will take a master to hurdle the earth-mind truth. But that is what you are about here, is it not? You give the truth to your mind that will make you a master. The writer is wrong that it will take a master to understand. It will, instead, **make** a master of the one who works to bring these truths into his being.

This chapter ends on this note. The entity who you are, the mind/spirit that responds to God-mind, is now ready to work with your teacher. We who send these words through the writer go on with the next chapter, but you, in your wisdom, know that you must not read ahead of your understanding.

The Tender, Gentle, Positive Thrust of God Energy

6

Am I ready to manifest God substance into the earth plane?

My teacher is very patient. He is also wise enough to thrust my questions into the open channel to God-mind where they are met with answers that lead me to further questions. "What is the significance of what I am learning?" I keep asking, and the answers cause me to search deeper and deeper within myself.

Part of me resists, as it always has, to the amount of time and work it takes to gain spiritual growth. "But without understanding, there is only the pebble on the beach," my teacher said. "With understanding, there is the incoming tide and the surge of the entering sea that brings greatness into being."

The Brotherhood continued with their message.

That which now opens to the readers of this book teams them up with the Being who reaches toward them with open arms. That Being is, of course, the God of the Universe. To receive this Gentle One, this Tenderness in Expression, this perfection beyond anything you ever thought of before, you must understand the lessons already learned. Therefore, do not reach forward to bring this chapter into your understanding until you work with the others.

Be entirely open with your teacher. Team up with this advanced master who wants to help you through this text. The work we plan to do in this book requires your highest truth, your best openness and your eternal generosity toward your gentle being who works to be a master. The writer wonders at the words "generosity toward your own being." But we say to you that unless you perceive yourself as having tenderness, you will be too harsh in your own approach to the work we do here. It is easy to become impatient. We see this already in the writer.

This one wants to accomplish all there is to understand in the time it takes to write about it. She thinks she may be one who can write truth, but not one who learns it well. You can easily see the lack of generosity she applies to her own being.

Therefore, we say to you, become patient and kind with yourself. Hold no animosity toward the reality of you — your spirit self — or toward your teacher who may never seem to be quite satisfied. Team up with the teacher and work to understand your own being who must unlearn even as you learn.

Be eternally open with the tender mercy that is given to you. Hand it out with great generosity. Team it up with those who enter your world to be the tender and compatible ones who help you to attain your goals. They will not waste this tenderness; they will not tread on it with unkind feet.

Your teacher arises each time you are ready to work, and it is this teacher's good will that is present in your relationship. There is no thought of tiredness or impatience on the part of a master teacher, nor is there any idea of being heavy hearted. Never think that you interrupt this one from more pleasant activities, for your teacher holds your being's growth as his greatest goal.

What else will give you reassurance? What more can we tell you that will open your mind to the task at hand? Go now with your teacher to hand over your trust in this advanced spirit who works with you. Go now with this advanced one to enter into the greatness that will be yours to work with in the earth plane.

Tenderness, which is part of God, is opposed to gaining and holding power over others, and it will not operate in this way. What we are trying to explain is that **to be a master of greatness, you must work with tenderness.** The manifestation of tenderness will be God truth. And the manifestation of God truth is the total good that opens to the earth plane.

Enter into new wisdom here. Open (your mind) to great hope and great eternalizations that will bring good into manifestation. Positive teamwork produces positive results. Positive tenderness will team up with the Gentle Being who is the God of the Universe. These two — tenderness and gentleness — hold you in the understanding which begins within the Mind of God. The Mind — the Truth Unleashed — the Greatness Manifested — these are all positive thrusts of power that begin in tenderness and unite with gentleness to be poured into the mold that you create.

Your mold is the eternalization that you hold in mind, reader! Team up with this understanding. The mold is that which you form in the temple of your being, that image that eternalizes the object that you want manifested. This eternalization produces the mold. The power of God produces the substance which unites with the mold when they wind together in tenderness and gentleness. This teamwork is of the utmost importance. Therefore, work with it over and over until you really do understand.

I interrupted to ask why I still resisted the concept of manifesting truth in the earth plane. My mind says I want to be a master of greatness, but there is also a voice within that nags at me to be reasonable — in the earth-mind sense.

You must make your eternalization before the God substance can adhere to the mold. This open truth is not like anything else you have been taught to believe. We know this is so, but we ask you to go beyond old truth, remember. We ask you to project our new truth and rise in spirit to enter into its understanding.

The mind we address when we address the reader is that which is spirit. The mind wants to work with real truth, not truth that is old and tired. In fact, the mind resists what is old and tired. Therefore, free your mind from its labors and let it soar. Team up with what we have already brought you in the way of truth — the new understanding regarding gravity, for example. Review this truth. Then enter into the other truths you have been working with. What holds you back from this progress is your thought of explaining to others how this works. We hear you (hear your thoughts) looking about at your neighbors and wondering how would you explain the presence of your projected thought. What would they say?

Laughter — mine — interrupted the flow of explanation. Thoughts paint us in our true colors. There are no secrets, and pretense or posturing is futile. Only honesty will do in our spiritual relationships with the God of the Universe, the Brotherhood and our teachers.

The Brotherhood continued with the text they bring through God-mind.

This work we enter into, this writing of truth, is not hard for us to understand because we who reside here in this next plane can see with true vision. You there in the earth plane probably have not become accustomed to seeing with truth. Therefore, you, along with the writer, probably tend to enter into the gentle reasoning that teams up with earth-mind. But never enter therein without reminding yourself that earth truth has not and cannot wrest this planet into its purity. Only the truth that we bring through the gentle being who opens her mind to us will be the truth that will work in the time to come.

Provide good in your environment by holding up this truth we bring to the Light of God. There you will see it for what it is — the perfection, the hope to be made manifest.

To team up with the eternalization we give you, put your mind into neutral, and let it stand as idle as possible. Give no information to your mind until you send it this one thought — **God enters. God is here in this place where I am.** Hold this image as long as you can.

Bring new hope to your mind by adding the idea that God enters to be one with this mind. Then wait.

Team up with this idea, this certainty of God and you — **one in purpose, one in mind.** Now bring your truth to the same place. Ready? Turn to your eternalization. Hold it before your mind. Throw each detail into the picture, and hold it there. Hold your understanding firmly in place.

Now turn open (use) the truth that God's power fills the vessel (mold) you provide. Your willingness to team up in the way outlined here shows the extent of your cooperation, and we open to you whatever it is you need most to accomplish your goal.

Present your being openly and with tender concern, getting the most of each word we give you. Present openly and fully a mind open to truth, open to God, and teamed up with tender notices that you will now become the truth in operation. Then we will open our beings to the fulfillment of the truth and put it into the earth plane as that which you have molded in your mind.

Be tuned in to us as we work gently, but ever so surely, toward our goal of helping you meet the requirements to become a master of greatness. The wresting of truth into the energy of earth is not particularly hard to do. The only part that ever concerns beginners is the truth that must be flung into the energy without reservation. Your best efforts are required here, and the best efforts of the God of the Universe meet your own efforts. That assurance is easily given and probably easily received. But the hard part is being willing to make the initial eternalization and then putting it out as a mold in which you expect to gather energy. Try it, however. Try it now. Gently, with certain movements, tenderly, with the best of your being united with God who reaches to present you with His power, privately within your own temple. That is the way, the means, the eternal truth.

Better energy has no hope of expressing, for the power of the God of the Universe is the most complete power available. The only other power enters through earth-mind which may express its final thrust of opposition here. Some old truth may reach forth to bring you notions of how ridiculous you look, or if it works, how will you explain what you have done? The earth-mind wants your attention, and it may give you its best and give you its worst at the same time. Eternal truth will prevail, however, for you have teamed up with the energy of the universe which teams up with the great gifts of God. Use this energy; hold no other thought of earth-mind truth. Thrust opposing truths away as you would push the enemy out of your house. Team up now and bring forth whatever you want to see.

Turn now to Universal wisdom on the matter of this planet. What do you want to put into this planet? What is your assignment? What will your specialty be? These questions need answers, and we ask you now to work with your teachers to learn these answers for yourself. When you have the answers, put them into the back of this book into the space allowed for such things. We, in turn, will write these same answers in our book of records where the open channel may reach forth to touch you with the need of your particular speciality.

I reread the chapter, worked within myself on several points, and after some time elapsed, I asked my teacher, "What is my assignment, my specialty?"

"To write the books, to help put the truth into the universe, to get the positive thrust of energy expressed in the world by doing whatever is needed to bring the books into the world."

I wondered if I should include my personal answer in this book.

"The reader can see for himself that your purpose is already established."

Finally, I asked if I should help restore this planet with God truth.

"The raising of good in the earth is the responsibility of each master, no matter what his personal assignment may be. The perfect alliance that is required between you, God, the Brotherhood and the earth plane requires the perfection of truth to be instated. Therefore, you, who writes books as an assignment, may also put good into expression in any way that is helpful to mankind."

The Brotherhood then continued with the chapter.

That which opens to you in the matter of your assignment or speciality and any other work that can be done is what you must concentrate on. That which is yours and yours alone opens you to the work you need to give attention to. The writer must concentrate on writing truth books, her specialty. You, the reader, must concentrate on whatever it is you have now learned is your assignment. We who watch over you have written into the record book the various assignments.

The writer wonders how we can handle so many names, so many assignments. The record books we keep are so named because they do enter whatever it is we need entered. But our methods and your methods on the earth plane are vastly different. The word processors we use have an open channel available, not the various inputs through other data from the earth data banks. We need only know how to enter the names, and the names are entered,instantaneously. And when we need the files on those who work with shelter, for example, we have them at instant recall. Why worry about how we send the truth to our records? When you come here we will explain it to you in person.

Enter into the work for which you are best suited, and in that way you will be successful in helping those who require your help in the New Age. Be open and receptive to the work you must do to attain the degree of master in your field. However, the time is not yet when you are ready to make the perfect manifestation of truth. Much needs to be done with your being as it assimilates truth. Also there is much to understand about the eternalizations that will thrust God power into the molds you create in order to channel the substance of God.

The eternalization we now open to you is of the student who brings truth into his being, the student who knows the work is worth the effort, worth the time and worth the optimum energy required. This eternalization we hold of you is to help you become a master of greatness.

Getting the Most Out of Your Earth Experience

7

How can I use Pure Truth experimentally?

The cry "Team up!" is given yet again. Those who organize this material believe candidates for master of greatness are now ready to put their truth on the line. They are to get on with putting the Pure Truth into material form in order to benefit mankind through their teamwork with the God of the Universe.

Exciting? Yes, and also demanding. So throw open the doors of your temple that you may work in tandem with those who have now put themselves to the task of helping all of us who have accepted the challenge of being candidates.

Team up with the God of the Universe, the Perfection, the Wholeness, the Wondrous Expression of all good. To become eternalized within this energy — which is God — is to be sure you enter into your greatest potential. Teaming up will bring you those qualities which are God Himself, and teaming up means you will express these qualities in your life.

Why team up with the idea that **maybe** God will help you? Why team up with the notions put forth by churches that God does not always give us good gifts? Why project the if's and the but's that cause you to recede from the greatest encounter ever?

Bring the earth-mind truth to an end, candidate. Trust in our words that will make your lifetime experience more than you ever thought possible. These hopes for goodness expressing in your life may be fulfilled. They may enter into fruition when you open yourself fully to God. This is why we give this subject a chapter at this point in the textbook. We really do not believe you enter into earth-mind truth to any great extent — at least not deliberately. But we want you to recognize those residues of corrupt thinking that can hurt your better understanding. To be a candidate for the master of greatness, you must know the truth and follow it without any reservations.

The Pure Truth that God brings to you, that which is yours and yours only, will lay before you the means by which you can bring the truth into manifestation. In other words, candidate for master of greatness, Pure Truth is that which is given to you only, to your mind, to your truth center. This particular truth will be yours to manifest in the earth plane, and **the God of the Universe will have then presented you with the truth and the means by which you may demonstrate it.**

I interrupted the transmission to ask if the Pure Truth has the inherent quality of manifestation. "If so, are you telling us that all we need do is to recognize this fact?" The answer came immediately.

That which you now see is because the understanding has reached you. The Pure Truth is, indeed, that which God pours out upon you, that which you can turn into earth material. Put the Pure Truth into the laboratory where you can explore its possibilities.

Laboratory? I went to my teacher for an explanation.

"Turn to the Truth of Purity, the truth that is given you to put into earth existence. Use it. That is what is meant."

This "laboratory" the Brotherhood mentioned — doesn't that suggest experimentation? May I think in these terms? May I try manifestation without thinking that somehow I have failed God if it doesn't work out as I think it ought?

The Brotherhood gave me further insight.

The writer enters into our word with great anticipation. And we hope the other candidates for master of greatness do likewise. The laboratory we have in mind is within your own being, perhaps housed within your temple somewhere where you get acquainted with new truth, new expressions of truth, new thoughts. This laboratory may be your secret place for working with the principles, the laws, the Pure Truth of your own being. Yes, we mean what we say here, and we invite you to experiment.

The writer tends to take things too seriously — especially herself. The Brotherhood want you all to relax, enjoy this work, team up with us in all matters, use the resource of your personal teacher. The idea of putting your truth to the test is not repulsive to God, nor does it mean you put your faith on the line to win or to lose. God tries again and again to help you to win. Earth-mind truth says that God will be angry if you cannot have perfect faith, but God is not interested in condemnation, only in growth. Would an earthly parent chastise a child who did not do a task perfectly the first time? Would a good earthly parent encourage, help, team up with, and otherwise hold up the child who is trying? Enter, then, into God truth with understanding and with gentleness. Remember the lesson of the previous chapter and handle yourself with gentleness.

Team up, my gentle one, team up to bring new growth into your soul. Give your being a chance to put truth into the earth plane. Give your own Pure Truth into objects that earth eyes can see. Team up within the laboratory you have now created, and let us go to work.

Teamwork is all important in this laboratory. The gentle presences here will open themselves to you to give you better opportunities to present the earth with good. Here is your teacher who has come to help. Others in the Brotherhood arrive, too, to help in the experiments. Then there is, of course, the presence of the Perfect One, the All in All, the God whose thoughts energize the eternalization you must make.

The scene is now painted in its true colors, and you are ready to embark on your experiment. Team up. Draw close to us. Give your attention to what you must do and be sure we will do what we must do. Put the thought of truth into the eternalization.

I turned to my teacher for help. How can I picture truth?

"Give your picture the wonderful tenderness that you hold for good. Be true to your own feelings of what is good."

I closed my eyes and meditated, reaching within to experience the gladness and the wonder of good in the world, any and all good that increases people's joy and deep happiness.

"Now join with that picture your own eternalization of some particular good that rises in your mind as making people happy."

I wondered if this good should be concrete or abstract? Should it be an inner joy — like many experience at Christmas? Should it be a tree in bloom? A building beautified? A manifestation of love such as a gift of money for the betterment of the city?

"The truth that enters you will tell you what to bring forth."

I puzzled over these words and then asked my teacher if my assignment — speciality — had something to do with what I manifest.

"The manifestation may be according to your specialty, but it may also be, remember, any good that you want to bring into the earth plane. Eternalize the object you have in mind. Hold it within your temple where you can detail it."

I stopped, even as you are stopping, to make the eternalization I decided upon.

The Brotherhood continued the explanation.

Eternalize the worth of the object you have in mind. Will other people benefit from it? Is this eternalization passing the generosity test? Is it passing the test of eternal truth in action? The eternal truth, remember, says that each good that is held openly in the eternalization will be brought forward into the material substance if held in the mind securely and with the thrust of power from God.

The writer opens herself to writing, and she thinks, too, of various ideas that will help people, but she has not yet opened herself to making the demonstration we call for. The truth we want everyone to call forth enters as your only power.

I interrupted to ask what was meant by the last statement.

The power enters with the truth, for God truth has power within it. The truth you want, therefore, that truth of God which you want to instate within the earth, will have the needed power within it to manifest **because it is of God.** You must now work with this understanding.

I stopped to confer with my teacher. "My mind is whirling. How can I focus on one truth to bring forth into my community or my neighborhood?"

"The truth you want to demonstrate must open your mind to the potential goodness that is possible. Therefore, team up with what is presented in this book. To gain power over earth material, remember that the God of the Universe eternalizes each activity. Therefore, you, who are of God, may also use this powerful thought."

After a review, I finally decided upon a certain dem-*onstration.*

"The God you hold in mind will team up with your idea when you know that truth governs the situation you have in mind. Team up with the total truth — not just part of it."

Had I chosen too hard a subject?

"Team up with power," came my teacher's answer. "That which holds you back from demonstrating is the idea you pursue way back in your mind that the demonstration is not possible, even for God!"

Was it true? Was I really thinking that God cannot do this thing? Winter weather had closed in on the day this chapter was written. Could that be the cause of my doubts? There was no way to escape the challenge, no way to put it out of my mind with outside activity. Ice pellets had fallen during the night, and even our dogs slipped and slid as they moved about.

"Team up with the God of the Universe," came my teacher's words. "Team up, team up, team up."

The message reminded me of the early days of my writing when I wanted so much to have a teacher from the next plane of life. I had waited, pencil poised, only to receive meaningless swirls and letters. After several sessions — 15 or 20 — came the words, "Team up." Over and over these words appeared, and along with them, "Open your mind."

Again I looked at the same words — "Team up." What more is required, I wondered. "That which comes to you — the work of the partnership — must be entirely within your understanding," was the message my teacher gave me.

The Brotherhood continued.

Your truth may express with power as you become the teammate of the God of the Universe. That which is "you" — your reality — teams up with the truth that God presents, the truth that enters to be taken into the present situation where you live, work and enter into perfection.

Therefore, turn now to your demonstration. Work with your teacher to understand and to eternalize exactly what it is you want. The truth that is yours is bound to the universal power, the universal substance and the universal God who eternalizes with you whatever it is that projects His good.

Go to your temple to review, if you need to do this. Go to your temple to gather your spiritual resources. Team up with the Perfect Teammate who wants to work with you. Become the truth in expression, candidate, the truth which opens to the earth to give what is valuable beyond compare.

The Quality of Tenderness — the God Self Expressing

8

Why is tenderness the catalyst of manifestation?

That which is of God is kind, merciful, gentle and totally loving. We call those qualities **tenderness.** You, who team up with God-mind, experience tenderness in the communication you receive from the One Who Is Tenderness in expression. You, who enter into your temple to receive your Pure Truth, know the perfect tenderness with which God-mind deals with you.

Therefore, we will now enlighten you about the way tenderness enters into your own demonstrations of Pure Truth. Gentle understanding is given you that you may understand why your own demonstrations must be presented to the earth in perfect tenderness, not in hasty turbulence or in angry thought. To express as God, you must use the very qualities which are of God. To wrest the truth into material form, you must use the perfection that is truly God. When you follow this plan, this truth, this understanding, you will not fail to put God-mind truth into the earth.

In the New Testament, I remembered reading that Jesus often went apart from his disciples to meditate and to be alone. Was he gathering his spiritual resources — the God qualities the Brotherhood mentions? I asked for a comment.

The one named Jesus entered into demonstration after demonstration because he did so with the totality of God expressing through him. To be able to maintain his God integrity, Jesus teamed up with God-mind to receive his perfect truth and to receive in abundance the understanding he needed to continue his work.

That he went off alone is not to be wondered at, for who among you can enter into God-mind and not know the essential base of its worth? The one named Jesus knew the tremendous value that God-mind brought; therefore, he went apart to receive this truth that he might team up with all that God had for him. He did not go because he was weary of well-doing. He went because he was thirsty for the truth.

The truth that God-mind brings is presented in terms you can understand, and it is perfect for you, as Jesus' truth was perfect for him. You, like Jesus, can put personal truth into expression in the earth plane, for you, like Jesus, team up with God-mind and the Brotherhood. The truth that enters your being may be put to use, but the truth of others is only to be used by them, not you. Therefore, to say to you as a group, "Do this, or try that," will not do at all!

Put on the entire mantle of God, not just the innovative teamwork that will take you to the well, so to speak. The only one who can drink deeply of truth is you, the candidate for greatness. The only one who can demonstrate with the perfection that is required is you, the one who now reads these words.

The point we make is that no one will receive the master of greatness degree unless he turns away from limiting opinions generated within. These opinions concern the wisdom of enacting truth or concern over how much energy and time this project is taking. When you turn to such thoughts, you enter into total limitation and team up with only the exterior posture of a candidate who never puts truth into motion.

Tenderness, the greatness quality which is the subject of this chapter, is that which you must cultivate as you would cultivate your personal earth garden. This quality encompasses several earth-named qualities (such as love, kindness and tolerance), but in itself it is wholly comprehensive. Therefore, concentrate on this word — **tenderness.**

Team up with what it is — God truth, God majesty, God persuasion. The word itself has powerful teamwork. That is, it holds great vibrations that will reach out to you who ready yourself to receive the word in its totality — its meaning and its authority over your own being. The truth here is that **tenderness has a truth of its own making.** The word inhabits the vibrational space that teams up with what is perfect, and you team up with this quality to become the one who masters the truth of manifestation. This word — in the truth sense — is your personal entry into the eventual consummation of your own good with God truth. The opening of your soul into this understanding brings you into this wonderful relationship between what you are and what God IS.

Be into our open truth here. Be into our message. Team up with your teacher to apply what we say here to your own being.

What a strong message! I asked my teacher to bring the meaning of tenderness into my own understanding.

"To truly understand," my teacher told me, you must take that word within you and meditate upon it. Hold it in your inner temple as you would hold a child who wants your tenderness. This tenderness wants you, Truth-Giver!

The Brotherhood continued.

Whatever your teacher suggests is to give your own spirit its personal truth in a way it can accept. To give each of you the same kind of picture would be foolish, indeed. Therefore, do not let this writer's teacher be your teacher's voice. Those teachers assigned to each of you know you intimately, and only they can help you through the experience we now encourage.

That which becomes your own truth is now ready to be made use of in a personal way. Team up with your best understanding of what you have learned, and turn yourself to producing the truth that you want to produce. Each of you now has an idea of what that truth must be. Each of you knows what to do to give the truth meaning and form within the earth plane. Therefore, do what you must, and accomplish your work within your gentle being who responds to truth as a moth responds to light.

Tend to your work. Pause here and begin the process. The laboratory awaits your use. Go within to make use of the optimum energy that comes toward you. Know that God-mind holds forth perfection. You will determine the objective by teaming up with the project, whatever it is, and entering into its optimum energy. Then open your mind to the quest — to the results. They must certainly form within the laboratory. They surely open to the world for all to see. They must stand forth as the truth manifested!

Step by step I followed the suggestions above. My eternalization, I thought, was clear enough. The perfection that I knew would occur teamed up with reality as I viewed it. I waited. That which I applied my truth to was not an object, but an objective. That which I targeted was not something that could be seen at once. What should I do next? I waited for my teacher's instruction.

"Team up with the truth entering the subject you chose. That which presents a barrier to your sight may disappear as you open your inner eyes, your eyes that now team up with truth. That which has now received truth has centered it within itself. That which has received the truth knows that truth has entered, and that it must respond."

In this way my teacher encouraged me. There was much more, of course, but the words were specific and to the point of my eternalization. Because it involves others, I cannot share what I have eternalized.

The Brotherhood continued.

The words that enter your mind from your teacher will be those that will help you to adjust your eternalization, if you must, or to hold it firmly in place, if that is the decision. Your teacher will work with you individually and will enter into your laboratory work with optimistic encouragement. Those who are teamed up with you know the process works — the process of using your truth to team up with God power to bring good into the earth plane.

The process of your eternalization may need review. Let's take time on this point. When teaming up with the energy within your laboratory, team up with the Pure Truth that is given to you, and you alone. Team up with this truth because you can make use of it in the earth energy. The truth that is yours will have its own power, its own thrust of energy that will be the creative force you need to make it enter the earth plane.

Give this Pure Truth your attention. Work with it in private. Then figure out how you can use it for good in your own community. The truth, remember, brings its own energy. When you use that which is just for you, we will be able to assist you better. When you reach out to get the truth of others and put this truth into the earth plane, you have dissipated the power. Give attention to that which is yours to give, not to the truth of others.

Enter into our best understanding as you give yourself to this experiment. What you now work with is not only possible, it is as sure as your walking to a friend's house and seeking a glass of water. You would not be reluctant, would you, to ask your friend for water? Then eternalize without fear. Put your truth out there and free your mind to perform the greatness of manifestation.

The writer seeks to express her truth in her own unique way, but it may not be your way. The writer wants to see the results, though it is hard to see results when the truth must express in others. That is why we have indicated to her that she may have to see past barriers that man erects, see into the hearts of those involved. Then she will know where the truth entered and how it affected those to whom she sent it. Her partnership is true; her picture is tender and gracious; her help to others is ready to manifest. There is no way to be that man or woman who teams up with God-mind truth and then turns to the earth-mind to finish the project. The one who turns to God-mind must stay with God-mind unswervingly. The earth-mind produces what earth-mind is capable of, but God-mind can accomplish the eternalization of truth!

Be turned toward the truth that God brings only to you. Enter into this truth and hold it within you. How can you put it to work in the world you live in? How can you demonstrate the truth that mankind needs and wants? How can your truth go forth on wings to accomplish what God wants? How can you put your truth into the eternalization of the perfection that you want to put forth? These questions need answers, candidates! These questions need your attention. They need your scrutiny, your analysis, your teaming up to receive answers. Team up with your teacher now to begin work.

Spiritual growth is not easy — at least not for me. "When you instate the truth within you," my teacher said, "you begin the growth process. But until you express your truth in material terms — that is, open your truth to the earth plane — growth is at a standstill.

"The truths that you want to instate within the earth plane may be placed there to enter into those who, like you, reveal their needs and their cries. Others can be filled even as you are filled. The entering truth is not just for you, but it is there for all you want to share it with."

The Brotherhood summarized the message of this chapter.

The truth within you is like a penny that you find lying on the street. The penny is not valuable in and of itself, but when you put it with your other pennies, it begins to indicate more value to you. "I can use this penny I found and all the other pennies to buy the thing I want most in all the universe," you say to yourself. "The penny that I found today will certainly contribute to the goal that I have of purchasing the greatest teamwork possible." The pennies sparkle with promise, and you consider the work you want done.

"I will get a team of workers," you say aloud, "who will team up with me to bring forth the wine from the grapes in the vineyard!" Then you open the box of pennies and count them, one by one. The truth here is that until you open the box, you only make promises to yourself, but when you open it, there is the reality. You count the pennies and then you put them in the bank. "I now have enough to pay my team of workers," you say, but the open box is empty.

"Where is the money?" the would-be workers ask when they enter your house. "Why," you say to them, "the money is safely in my bank. You will get paid after you work." But the workers' needs are great, and they want money now, not later. But you insist that they work first. The workers, uncertain of your reliability, turn to some other open door to find what they need.

Insight from the Brotherhood into the meaning of the parable opens it more fully to our understanding.

The pennies are those truths you enter into your mind where they brighten the atmosphere. These pennies, or truths, are carefully hoarded, but not spent. You who team up with the value of these pennies, or truths, lose the benefit they might bring you. That is because you refuse to spend them until you can see with your eyes and know in your mind that the truth manifests in the earth plane. Therefore, your opportunities for putting the truth into the earth plane fall away and your chances to participate in greatness pass you by.

Those of you who hoard your truth, put it in the safe deposit box of your mind and refuse to team it up with the needs that you see in the earth, will only have truth, nothing else. There will be no truth blossoming into earth matter, no truth developing into meeting the needs of those in the earth plane. No, you will only have what you started with — nothing more. And you will never be a master of greatness.

To let go of your truth and to put it into the earth plane you must team up with tenderness, for it is this quality that pushes the truth out to meet the needs of earth. This wonderful tenderness is the essence of what God IS. And tenderness is the essence of what you are, candidate for the master of greatness. Therefore, hold this wonderful tenderness within you that you may open your treasure chest to express greatness, not to store what is within in some far and safe place where it will help no one.

This is the thrust of our message that is now open to you who must study it with care. That thought of tenderness, remember, is your key to opening your own being to enter into the perfect teamwork with the wonderful God of the Universe.

You Can Grow Beyond Your Plan

9

How can I determine my potential?

The truth you reach for, the truth God-mind affords you, will open your earth existence to wonderful, creative endeavors. The truth you brought to planet earth, truth you learned during other lifetimes, is ready to be put to use.

Your being has no limits, no restrictions. We never say to you, "The truth you already have is enough. Team up with that and no more." We always leave the optimum possibility open to you that you may in any lifetime team up with your potential and give to earth all that it is possible for you to give. Holding open your potential is how you grow, how you join with whatever is possible in your lifetime existence.

The openness with which you team up with this truth will be the gauge by which you can view your results. Teaming up with what we say, without reservations, will make your being quiver with anticipation because you will know the thrill of putting truth to work.

The estimated worth of your truth cannot be determined because whatever it is will not be readily apparent. To evaluate truth either in dollars and cents or any other coin value is to touch only the surface of what is possible. Whatever truth you take into yourself may be put into the earth plane, so who is to say now what that value is?

To properly know what we mean, you must now eternalize, as you eternalized before. But this time you must put whatever truth you have into the earth plane without any hesitation. Here is how you can work with this idea. Know what truth you most enjoy or team up with. What is it? Name this truth before your teacher. Then team up with the teacher to voice not only the truth but what you think you might do with this truth in the earth plane.

I paused, thinking of the law that ***all truth must manifest in the earth plane.*** *My teacher tells me frequently that "the wresting of your truth into the visible is not only possible, it is the law."*

How could I use my truth for the benefit of others? I stared out the window. My teacher's words came to me. "That which you produce must enter the earth plane through your own understanding of how truth works, not through my understanding. Therefore, step forth to view the earth around you. The environment where you are — is it perfect? The teaming up of truth with matter — where would it benefit the most people?"

I looked around me. It was a sunny February day, and the temperature was 58 degrees F. My husband was on the golf course; our golden retriever was enjoying a roll in the grass. People looked prosperous, happy. What could I possibly add to the environment on such a day?

"Give your truth away," came my teacher's answer. "You can give gifts in the midst of abundance. Why wait for a need? Team up with your truth to give a gift right now on a beautiful winter day when the lifetime experience appears very good."

So it was up to me to begin the process. "The truth is yours, not mine, to give," came my teacher's words.

The Brotherhood resumed the chapter.

The openness with which you receive your teacher's advice teams up with your success in the manifestation of your gift. Therefore, open your mind to this one who enters to help you to bring the truth into manifestation.

Those in the Brotherhood of God enter their own truth to you to help you know the wisdom of what we bring to you. We hold our truth out to you to help you eternalize what we tell you here. The words are only words until you grasp their meaning, their perfect truth, their teamwork that will instate truth right where you are in the God self that lives in the body. Reach for the wisdom of what we tell you. Reach for the energy with which to master the procedure. We hold it out to you . . . and you . . . and you.

I frequently take deep breaths just to relax, to quiet myself while I work with the truth that often comes in torrents. There is much to learn, to understand and to apply.

The writer teams up with her own self-consciousness because she wants to place her own truth into the work place of earth. The truth she works with is the truth that goes forth to those in the earth plane who want to know open truth for themselves. As a result, she enters into so many writing projects that she whirls about to get it all completed. Then she wonders why she is not putting her truth to work in the earth plane.

What she must do, and what you, the candidate, must do is to understand what it is you can best give to the earth plane. The writer thinks in terms of truth to help people live their lives. You may think in terms of an abundant food supply or the worth of the entity who needs new ways of making money. Each candidate will think differently, work independently, but will use truth to accomplish the ends held in mind. The writer thinks constantly of new books — books for adults, books for children, and these books that are her special assignment. Her mind revolves with ideas for putting truth into the marketplace where people can have the product.

One person does one task; one does another. Do not think you must do what another does. The object here is to use the truth that comes to you. Use this truth to team up with God power that will put your truth into an earth form that can be used, read, eaten, given for pleasure and on and on. Team up with what you most want to give; do not think you must dredge up some other plan.

Frankly, I received the above message with relief. I understand that the message of truth needs to be spread far and wide, and my own truth wants to project into many, many books for people of all ages. I do what I do best and others do what they do best.

The Brotherhood continued.

That which enters now is truth that comes through the open channel from God-mind. We who are teaching in this way want only to bring truth that will give you the perspective you need to enter into the work of putting truth into the earth. What more can we say to you to convince you that each of you has a truth to give, a truth to instate and enter into the very form which earth will take into itself?

The writer is an example of one who puts her truth into the form that earth accepts. But there are others at work, too. There is a man in the eastern part of the world where the tenderness of God is not known. This man, who has heard his own truth, wants to instate tenderness in ways that people will understand and accept. Therefore, he generously provides the eternalization of vast value to each person by teaming them up with the tender understanding of how a country can grow if its people are well and hardy. This man teaches through his eternalizations that people are divinely appointed by God to give good back into their country.

By teaming up with God power, this man has opened the country to giving great care to its pregnant women, its children, and the youth who arise from the land ready to serve it. There is a growing regard in this place for the earth itself, to its bounty that may prosper them if they protect it and help it to serve those who live there.

What is happening there is minuscule by earth standards, but by the standards of God-mind, the work is mammoth in size, tremendous in scope and is an example that can lead a troubled world into tender understanding for this entire planet.

There is another example going on at the present time in another part of the planet. This group of people have taken the light of God into their laboratory. There they learn how to contribute to the planet in eternalizations of perfect production of the crops that can grow even where the land has not been hospitable. This laboratory is not secret, yet it is virtually unknown to others. Why? Because people write off the value of what they see in such ordinary surroundings. There is no great funding for the project. No, there is only the vision that several agricultural scientists hold and work with in their homemade laboratory. By earth standards this project is worth little, but by the standards of God-mind, this laboratory is the heart of Pure Science that emanates through the perfect Mind of God.

The writer wonders if there is anything an individual can do alone. What if, she wonders, a person reads this book and is not scientific, is not even certain what kind of needs he or she might meet. What can this person do? The person she describes enters into the work of others even though this solitary individual may not know it. Here is how this works.

The person who has been productive in life, but is now, perhaps, aged in body, may think he or she cannot lead a team of scientists. But the reality of the situation is this. If science is your understanding and your interest, you undoubtedly have ideas on how to help this planet and its people. Hold that idea in mind, eternalize it and send it on its way in as complete a form as you can. This eternalization will go to the open mind of another who may be able to enact your own eternalization. The second individual will say to others, "Why, this idea came to me in a dream!" Or he may say, "This thought came to me full blown on how we can purify our water supply!" He may never know that the inspirational thought he received came from one who knew the answer, but felt that it was not possible to execute it by himself.

This means, as the writer is now excitedly noting, that everyone everywhere in all kinds of conditions may serve up answers that can help our earth to prosper, and along with the earth, the people who live there.

The Brotherhood was right about my excitement. How many times have I heard intelligent people outline what was to them the perfect answer to great problems on this planet. Others, listening, nodded in agreement. But then someone made that limiting statement, "But what can one person do?" Then, the same individual or someone else added a decisive, "Nothing!" Now we know that there is no such thing as "only one person." Our individual minds are capable of sending out ideas into open minds anywhere.

Any mind that enters into the Pure Truth of God-mind has the powerful teamwork that goes with that greatness. Therefore, when you, a candidate for greatness, reach out with your full blown God thought, the thought will not be wasted upon the minds of those who turn only to earth-mind. Those who immerse themselves in earth-mind cannot perfectly understand God-mind thought, for to them, the earth is what the earth eye sees, what the earth body experiences. Then how does the mind of such a person gravitate toward what is of God?

The wisdom that people think is immersed in earth-mind is better lost than heeded. To perpetuate that which is ancient wisdom is to perpetuate what is not the answer to give to earth today. Therefore, why turn to such old, old truths that by now have the dust of the ages upon them? To reunite earth with the bright light of creativity, one must work with the truth that pours through the entire universe, truth that is broadcast through the minds of individuals like yourself. To enter into God-mind is to reunite with Light. But to turn back the old curtains to what was once thought to be wisdom is to reunite with the truth that brought the earth into its present condition.

Understand this. Know that you, whoever you are in the scheme of the universe, may be the master of greatness who will turn the tide of events upon this earth by bringing goodness into perfection, goodness into the visible and concrete earth form. There need be no restriction upon this statement that will apply to you. Hold no restrictions for your being, candidate. What is possible through God is now possible through you. This is the truth we bring you here, not a fantasy or a statement of utter ridiculousness. Those in the Brotherhood and the Source of Wisdom want you to take us at our word for what we bring you through this writer. You, candidate for greatness, can now weigh your truth and know its worth.

The truth you have may be used in endless ways, for endless needs, for endless problems, for endless creative projects. You, candidate for greatness, can be God in expression. Be teamed up with this understanding. You, the one who reads these words, are God in expression. We in this Brotherhood open ourselves to you, spirit to spirit, ready to help you to maintain this vibration in your life experience.

Your Partnership with God

10

What must I know to make my partnership with God the center of manifested truth?

Put your partnership with God into the teamwork that is positive and true. This partnership is just what it sounds like it is — that powerful teamwork that produces whatever is needed in your world. Partnership with God is not presumptuous, nor is it anything you should hide from because of some idea of humbleness on your part. This partnership is true, not a would-be hope. This partnership is workable, not a pie in the sky sort of statement. Therefore, open your mind, your heart, and put the truth within you into this thrust of eternal power.

Yes, the partnership with God is not just an individual truth that comes to some. It is eternal truth teamed up with universal law. God pushes truth into an expression that mankind can see, touch and hold. The partnership operates, but when you know how it works, why it works and the truth behind it, you can make it the center of your active participation in manifested truth.

This writer thinks these words bring forth a powerful response. They do, indeed! The power of the God of the Universe is no mean thing! This power works in the eternalization of truth that you make, whether or not you know of it. But when you do know of it, you can be more active than you have ever been in the expression of truth.

Bring your thinking into this chapter. The eternal truth requires your thought applied to it. When the God of the Universe is mentioned here, we are talking about **law,** not any religious tradition, not any team of philosophers who bring their thoughts to you. The **law** is that which IS, just as God IS. To understand our meaning, listen carefully to what we say.

Better truth than this partnership is not possible. To understand it fully, you must practice the principle. Teamwork will give you perfect understanding and perfect acceptance of the law or principle which is instated within the universe. Therefore, practice what is given here.

Put your heartfelt thought into the ether that comes to you. Put the ether, the substance which God provides you, into motion by teaming up with God. What do you think of? What do you want to give to the earth, to its people, to the New Age? To team up with God, there are two requirements. They are **the perfect eternalization of your thought and the application of the God principle that says that the teamwork of you and God together can work the ether into earth reality.**

Be sure you have these in mind — the eternalization and the partnership. Then, because we know you are each different, we ask that you work with your teacher to be sure your eternalization is that which you firmly believe in.

My own teacher responded to my question about my eternalization. "To be powerful in this thought that you send forth into the form of eternalization, give it the test of worthiness. Is this eternalization that which will help many people? Will it help them without regard to their own being — whether or not that being is helpful to you, for example?"

Since I could answer "yes" to both questions, I decided my eternalization was appropriate.

The message from the Brotherhood continued.

The way to be sure you are not offering ungenerous eternalizations is to hold this positive thought in the temple of your being where all is spirit. There is no materiality in your temple, no wealth that earth affords which can penetrate the place built within you for the spiritual work of your being. When you hold the thought there, it will certainly fade if it is merely for personal physical gain. The picture that stays has the worth of your truth in it.

The eternalization, once determined, must be polished brightly until it shines forth into the ether as that which must certainly enter into the world itself. This eternalization will not want to stay in the ether because of two things. First, truth must manifest! Second, the being you are in reality has teamed up with the God of the Universe to eternalize whatever it is that will bring great value to people. Therefore, it will go forth as the projected vision has produced it.

When you have completed this eternalization, when you have put it to the test, when you have solidified it by the perfecting that always must be done, then watch the ether generate the open truth that goes immediately to become matter! There will be no long time wait. God's partnership provides power, not vague whispers of promise. God's promise projects reality into matter, not reality into energy which may or may not express due to some worthiness or unworthiness on your part. When you have this understanding well in mind, you will begin to put truth into the earth right and left!

There is no reason to become too serious here! The open truth is great fun to work with. Hold your being open to this truth and race with your Partner to put it immediately into the earth. Would you put found money on the dining room table to look at and to get opinions about? No! You would race for the bank to put it safely away while you decided how to spend it.

Think of the open truth as found money. Put it safely in the bank of your temple where you eternalize it into the bright earth resource that will benefit people. The **inner** that we speak of is the spirit which is real, and the **outer** we express is the earth substance that teams up with eternalizations.

In your earth teamwork, don't you use the open lines of communication between you and other people? Then know that your communication with God is equally important when working with Pure Truth. Turn your mind to God-mind truth, open yourself to its reception, team up with this One who wants to know you intimately. Ask questions you need answered, present tender requests you want granted. Put the certainty of your partnership above all other considerations. **The perfection of your truth, the perfection of your eternalizations all depend on this partnership.** Therefore, keep it the ongoing, bright and well polished vehicle for your use.

Be into the teamwork, too, of the Brotherhood. We only want to help you to be a master of greatness. That goal is now our chief concern, our worthy desire. That which opens to you through these words is what we want to give you. When we can help, through explanations, through the teamwork that we have together, we are here for you. The teacher you now work with will explain our role in your life.

My teacher said, "The Brotherhood has existed to be the arm of God which can communicate with you who live in the earth plane. Those who unite with you whenever you wish team up not only with you, they team up with God. There is no motive on their part except to help you arrive at your spiritual goal — to be one with God. Theirs is not a labor of eternal hardship; theirs is a labor of true tenderness in expression. Therefore, you who need help of any kind know you can go to the Brotherhood to have the entering truth presented to you."

The Brotherhood resumed the chapter.

The energy that comes to the earth plane is entered through the wonderful thoughts that open to the understanding of the God of the Universe. These thoughts that go out to God, your Partner Who is bound to you in spirit, team up with great energy that encircles the world. Each God-thought you send forth is the energy that opens itself to this world we all hold very dear. To be more conscious of this process, you might try an experiment.

In the laboratory where you work, perhaps your inner temple, you can see this for yourself. To put the energy to work, think "God." Let your thought linger on the word, the thought that the word generates.

The word vibrates when you think it, when you pour your concentration upon it. The word seems to disappear, but it actually turns to energy. This energy will release itself as you think on the word once again until there is a tremendous buildup of energy. Then focus that energy upon the projected good. The writer has a bodily need right now. She can focus that energy upon that need. Another may know of the need of another person, and you may concentrate that energy buildup upon that person. This is how it works, the energy that you can generate with the help of your Partner. Then you can focus it through mind thought wherever or to whomever you wish. This sort of thing, remember,only works when two are perfectly teamed — the one who understands the nature of God and God.

Team up with the Partner who is your totality. Team up with the Partner who opens the door to positive results with your eternalizations. Team up with the Partner who now enters your laboratory to view the experiments you are working with. Team up with the Partner who enters with the truth — the truth that you might consider as the financial backing of your project. In the earth plane there must be coin of value to further enterprises. With this eternalization, the coin of value is the Teammate who enters into partnership with you.

Be assured of results when you throw all caution to the wind and depend upon the greatness of your Teammate's contribution to your project. This One is to be depended upon. This One is to be given perfect trust. This One has the positive power of the universe at command, and therefore, that which you eternalize is in the great hands that mold and produce the truth into earth form.

To work with your Teammate in an experiment is not to hold the relationship lightly, candidate for greatness. To experiment is to show wisdom, to show the opportunity and the understanding in a meeting point. Bring yourself to this understanding quickly that you may get on with your work. The one who is your teacher will help you at this point. This master of greatness will team up with you to help you across the bridge of concern, of doubt, of energy that fritters itself away. Your teacher will help you to gather your resources and plunge ahead into the perfect alliance with that One Who now enters to be your perfect Partner.

Be into this which we present to you. Be into perfect understanding. Be into eternal truth that tells you that **truth must express.** Then you will be into the Pure Truth that your Partner brings you, the truth that engages your mind, that pours into your being, that enters to be manifested.

Helpers Abound on the Next Plane

11

How do spirit helpers aid me in becoming a master of greatness?

No thought offers more power to your eternalization than the thought that you do not work alone, but in the midst of those who eternalize with you. There are, in this plane of life, millions of helpers who stand by to enter into the earth plane to assist those who want assistance. Your understanding of this support opens you to vast new horizons because the aloneness those in the earth plane find so appalling is not true.

Those in this plane who have prepared themselves to assist you in your work as a candidate team up with each request for more power. Those who stand by know how to work with you. They enter into the space you provide for them in your plane. But if you provide no space, offer no teamwork, they only wait in this plane to hear your tender call.

Therefore, when you work with what we have been teaching, the truth that enters through God-mind, you may have the help and counsel you desire. To find perfect understanding among others living on earth is unlikely, is it not? Those around you may think what you are doing here is interesting, even fascinating.

They may admire you. But how can they help? They may only hinder by giving limiting expressions to you, expressions that team up with earth- mind truth. They may say, "This idea you have sounds great. But people won't accept it!"

What does it matter what people accept? The perfect truth that enters through God-mind needs no acceptance by others. The perfect truth is that which stands on its own because it teams up with the power and authority of the entering greatness. If you must take polls to determine whether or not to go ahead with your study, you will not be a master of greatness.

Your only helpmate in the study upon which you have embarked is the teacher you now have and those who will assist in any way needed. Therefore, enter into this study knowing that your help does indeed come to you through the mind/soul, not through those in the earth plane.

Give your best attention to this plane. To invest yourself in this association is to learn what must be learned if you will move further into this study. The work of the spirit is not entered into earth; only the work of the body is entered there. To manifest truth into visible substance, spirit must work with spirit. The one you really are, the spirit self of you, must indeed work with us in this plane in order to put truth into the earth itself. Those of us who work with you have the perfect view of your plane, your earth situation. We here can help you there to reinstate truth where it is needed, and we will team up with you to accomplish this work.

That which now offers itself to you will eternalize the new earth and will help in the New Age. Teaming up with us will help those of you who remain in the earth plane to eternalize what is needed and what is helpful to the earth. You must hold yourselves in clear attention to our present association. That way you will not enter into bad thoughts of fear, of great anguish over change, over the perfecting of earth that will seem horrendous to many. Our present association will keep your mind clearly centered, eternally positioned to bring helpful thoughts into manifestation.

Give your time to our entering thoughts, to our presence, to our great help. By turning now to this plane, to these here who can help you, you will be able, in the times of great distress, to call on us with ease and with alacrity.

My thoughts went to mankind's present needs, present circumstances. How can we can use this helpfulness in our daily lives? The answer came immediately.

The way to bring this assistance into everyday use is to put this thought within your being — that each person has access to whatever help he needs. The writer fell down in the street and painful repercussions resulted. She was stunned, entirely consumed by pain. But in the midst of the pain, she called, "Brothers, help me."

The cry was the open door we needed. Those who could help her most entered her presence and began to work with her. The eternalization came immediately that the pain was subsiding, that the injury would soon heal, that everything was entering into wholeness. The injury took a while to heal because she holds to earth thoughts, and she expected the injury to heal by bits. However, when she teamed up more fully, we helped her to see progress every day, and she began to move with great energy toward the healing.

The story above is accurate. The injury was to a knee that was injured many years ago. The kneecap subsequently was removed. The pain from this new injury was consuming. I did call out quietly as the story indicates. The fall came a week and a half before a trip to Washington, D.C., and by the time I made the trip, I could bend my leg ninety degrees and there was no swelling. Within another two weeks, I moved about easily and resumed my long walks.

That is one example, of course, but there are many more. The writer is only one person, one entity, but when you who read this book team up to live your life by working daily with us, you will not even touch the earth but what you feel the presence of another who touches it with you. This partnership, this teamwork, is part of the eternal truth that is yours to make use of. You will not be alone in the work you now do.

The writer is thinking that never being alone seems rather horrendous to consider because she likes to be alone. The partnership of those in the earth plane and those in the next plane of life is totally compatible, not given to the grating and grinding of earth entities who are not compatible. Therefore, team up with us freely, knowing with certainty that those who will work with you have the true teamwork, the better understanding.

When those who open themselves to your requests team up with you, they will generate power that will keep you encouraged, keep you energized, keep you positive and active. You will respond with the authority of one who knows the truth that surpasses whatever has gone before. Put your trust in those who ready themselves for a new adventure in the earth plane. Give them your eternalization, your good thoughts that welcome them within your temple and that you are preparing yourself to work the seeming miracles in the earth plane.

Be the true teammate, the one who opens entirely to the powerful helpers who now want to be included in the work of rehabilitating both earth and mankind. Open to those who know the way to every good, the way to the perfect truth, the perfect understanding.

Give yourself time to work with those who open themselves to you. Team up as you become able to hold the thought in mind that the helpers are there to be called upon. Vast resources appear with those who now enter at your call, resources that even this textbook cannot begin to teach you about. Those who hold the keys to the kingdom of powerful resources know how to put these great resources to work, and they will not put them at the disposal of any but masters. Those who have no true understanding of greatness cannot possibly work with it.

Those who pour themselves into the work of greatness hold the key to power. They who turn to the helpers know the truth of their beings, the truth of the better way. Greatness manifests throughout the world among those who turn to helpers to give the truth power. Those who demonstrate the open truth generate power to bring truth into being because they use the resources of those advanced ones in the next plane.

The eternalization of better ways to bring the earth into balance now receives much power. The eternalization of ways to generate better health also receives power. The outstanding truth teams up with outstanding resources — gifts based on the laws and principles of the God of the Universe. In this way it comes together to become manifested truth.

Be truth in expression, masters of greatness, be truth that must become the eternalization of perfection in the earth plane. Team up with those who know the resources, those who want only to help the truth do its work of reinstating itself in the earth.

The Projected Reality

12

What is my responsibility in bringing God truth into material reality?

That which teams up with the earth is your own open truth. So you may not wonder at what is said here, we will direct the explanation in ways you will understand.

Be teamed up with what is of God — the goodness, the understanding, the eternal truth that abounds. The truth will team up with all that you think, all that you want expressed in life, all that is necessary and good to produce. Why does this happen? Because you are the eternal truth in expression!

Yes, you are that eternal truth because you have become the open minded individual who eternalizes that which is truth, that which enters through God-mind, that which reveals the way spirit works. This open mind of yours now eternalizes eternal truth, and therefore, you are the eternal truth in expression.

The writer is trying to cope with this explanation we have presented to you, but she still has some difficulty. Therefore, we will present it in another manner.

By the entering truth ye will know them. Yea, the way to the earthly kingdom is hard and difficult, but the way to eternal kingdoms is paved with the eternal gold of truth.

Not everyone will enter into this explanation, but we include it for those who prefer the biblical style. Those who recognize the tone may open their minds to the understanding. Those who recognize the allusions to certain Bible passages will either think this explanation is truly eternal truth or they will be puzzled, as the writer is puzzled.

In the Bible Jesus is quoted as saying, "Ye shall know them by their fruits." (Matthew 7:16 — King James), but we say, "By their entering truth ye will know them." The fruits of old meant the greatness of God manifesting in the earth plane. The truth enters people to be made manifest, and we think the word "truth" is more to the point.

Some are teamed up with the Bible explanation that says, "Enter ye in at the strait gate: for wide is the gate, and broad is the way, that leadeth to destruction, and many there be which go in thereat." (Matthew 7:13 — King James.) These words were a warning to people who would not keep their thinking in line with reality. The part about the narrow gate was meant to signify the easy way, the way that is easy to see and easy to follow. The wide expanse is the hard way, for it does not cut a clear path. That is its meaning.

The writer indicates that she has never heard this explanation of these Bible passages before. Perhaps the truth was somehow perverted; we are not sure. But we do know that the way to express truth is the way that is true, the way that is eternal, the way that is easy to follow. Why? Because the truth enters to guide you.

The projected reality is, of course, truth that has become material. This projected reality is earth reality, and is produced, not by hard work and not by the sweat of the brow, but by the truth itself which you project into the earth plane. Accept our explanation and become part of the truth that works the seeming miracle of putting the projection into the earth plane.

How can we speak with this great authority? Team up to learn how this comes about. None who open to our gentle truth will turn away to become less than masters of greatness. We who bring you this truth and those who work with you as individual teachers, one to one, will certainly be expected to bring the truth of God-mind! Team up to learn how you can project with great beta waves of creativity.

As an aside to the writer came the words, "Great truth is always hard to bring into focus, Truth-giver!"

The words about beta waves were ricocheting off the walls of my inner temple, and the Brotherhood, sensitive to my every thought, noted my agitation.

The writer twirls the words in her mind, but she does not reject them! The one who gives these words to you must work with her own teacher to learn the answer to what she asks, even as you, the reader, must ask your own teacher for help in understanding.

The beta waves are those waves of energy which eternalize whatever truth you want to project into reality there on earth. Not hard to understand, is it? Those of you who resist need to seek your teacher for more help at this point. Others may go ahead with this chapter.

The hope is that you will undertake the whole truth, not a part of it, for only by working with the whole can you put the truth into projected reality. Therefore, use your teacher to help you understand what is written here. Team up with the one who can help you in individual ways — the thing we cannot do in this book. Your teacher will help you sort it out — truth, the projection and the reality. There they are — the key words to understand.

Now let us focus on the next part of the chapter. Put your mind into neutral, for to try to absorb all that is said is futile. Just keep your mind open and receptive, reader, and turn the eternal truth into the perfect understanding.

Generous teamwork eternalizes whatever you want to project. We in the Brotherhood, the perfect Teammate — the God of the Universe — and your own reality or mind/spirit generate a teamwork that is greater than the total majesty of the universal union itself!

I struck the question mark several times. What does this last sentence mean?

The total majesty of the universal union is that which the God of the Universe holds in focus. But when we add the teamwork of spirit/mind that pushes forth to work as one with God, the strength increases to wrest the truth into the open marketplace of the earth plane. Yes, God is the Teammate Who makes the truth respond to its orders, but unless we who energize the projection act, there is no projected reality.

Those of you who still think that God acts without the help of mankind absolutely need to review **The Trilogy of Truth.*** God IS, mankind enters each lifetime to bring truth to life. God IS there for you; but if you ignore this Greatness, this Majesty, this Wonderful Good, the projected reality never gets underway.

Therefore, understand that the teamwork of all concerned means that whatever you place in your truth projection will form itself in the earth plane. The plan is intact. The plan is eternal. The plan will work if you do your part. Truth must manifest or it is the same as seed that falls upon barren ground. You are the ground, of course; the seed is the truth. The teamwork is the proven path to follow if you would capture the way to manifest tender truth upon the earth.

There was a woman in the earth plane who raised the biggest apples in her country. The other apple growers wanted to know how she got them to grow so big. The woman spread her arms to encompass the entire orchard, and she replied, "These apples seem big to you because your own apples are so small! But my apples only grow to their potential, do they not? Then why ask me why these apples do what the truth expected of them? Instead, ask yourselves, why do your apples reach only part way to their goal? Team up with truth, apple growers! The truth will set the standard; the apples will respond."

Those who understand the meaning in this parable will grasp the truth of this chapter. The truth is there to be used. The ones who project their truth into reality only do what is normal and good. Those who do not project the truth do what earth-mind directs, and the truth of earth falls short of the goal, as it always will.

Be entirely open to what is said here. Open your mind which will process this chapter's truth into your inner temple. Eternalize this truth until it is one with you, and then you will be another step closer to your goal of becoming a master of greatness.

*__The Trilogy of Truth,__ by Jean K. Foster; *The God-Mind Connection,* 1987; *The Truth that Goes Unclaimed,* 1987; *Eternal Gold,* 1988.

Teteract Truth — That Which Offers No Reward

13

How can we recognize God truth in every situation?

Whatever pushes itself onto God-mind truth to eternalize hopelessness, discouragement, teamwork gone amiss, we name "teteract." The master of greatness must acknowledge it for what it is, the eternalization of what is given by earth-mind. When you recognize it, you will not likely consider it worth your time and energy.

The "teteract truth" is able to sway many people because it has grown stronger through the years. Its strength comes through those who perpetuate it, those who insist on the earth truth as the ONLY truth worth heeding. The teamwork that gives people heavy hearts comes from this kind of truth. Troubles that magnify themselves without solutions team up with earth truth and offer you only hopelessness.

The opposite of "teteract" is "peterstet." The "peterstet" truth always satisfies, sees problems through to their perfect solutions — to the eternalizations that will bring you perfect results. These two words we use are not in the dictionary, as the writer often tells us. But their designations open the understanding so perfectly that we continue to use them.

This is the best way to prepare you, we think, for the days ahead when your involvement with the New Age will place you in new situations, new teamwork. Wetness (discouragement) will spread over the bright truth now and then, and you will think you are immobilized, that you cannot push through to accomplish the heavy work load you have. But know this wetness for what it is — "teteract" truth.

Greatness is possible only if you can relate to "peterstet" truth. Put yourself into this understanding. Put your being into association with this word we use that you may recognize it when it is given to you. New energy pushes through the wetness of discouragement when you say to yourself, "This that I feel is only the 'teteract' truth that tries to hold me back. There is no room in the New Age for 'teteract' truth. The 'peterstet' truth is mine to receive, mine to hold, mine to put into place in the earth plane." This reminder will be enough to put your mind into contact with what is truly God- mind energy.

I asked how "teteract" discourages us. Here is the answer.

'Teteract' truth eternalizes itself before your inner eye. It beckons you to follow its lead. This kind of truth brings itself to your mind with great self importance because it has received much honor from those in the earth plane. This truth very nearly **says** that it is the highest and the best. What is worse, there will always be those who agree.

Teaming up with "teteract" truth will bring you earth results that have been plaguing mankind since people turned away from "peterstet" truth. The earth truth is not poor because everything material is poor. The reason earth truth stands there in its ignorance of the better way is that mankind has put "teteract" truth in place of "peterstet" truth. Now, candidate for master of greatness, you must turn this business around! It is your time to put perfect truth back into earth, perfect truth we call "peterstet."

Eternalize within your being the pure "peterstet" truth. Hold this word within your being. Blend your understanding with it. When you find yourself wavering, find you are uncertain or uneasy about the work of the master of greatness, you will be attuned to our message. We will simply enter one word — "peterstet." Then you will know that you need the Pure Truth that only God- mind enters. "What?" you will ask us, "Am I returning to 'teteract' truth? Is that what is wrong?" We will give you simple assurance that you understand the matter.

The reason we make much of these particular words is that many times you will meet emergencies. In such times you may become anxious or given to worry, and you may easily revert to what you once believed — the "teteract" truth. Therefore, we want to use simple words which will get your attention and put you on the right track.

The Pure Truth you receive through God-mind always satisfies, always teams up with what is God. Therefore, never hesitate to be the requester, the one who wants God truth for every situation. Remember, the requester does more than ask for his own needs. The requester, in your case, receives truth that will help the many who cannot reach for this truth on their own. But they will not remain ignorant. You, the master of greatness, will help them to form their own open channel that they may use the resources of this plane.

Those of you who understand realize that your responsibility is putting God truth into motion on the earth plane. This work is yours to do and yours to explain to others. This responsibility will team up, however, with whatever you require in the way of energy and wholeness. To do this work, eternalize your own body as the epitome of good health, the epitome of buoyant energy. Heed this necessary eternalization that you will not become weak in body and thus open yourself to problems. Those who need you will be greatly disturbed if you fall into poor health. They think of you in the halls of the best of mankind, and they believe you hold the key to whatever is good.

They will not believe what you teach if you allow your body to fall into disarray. Therefore, team up daily with those who will help you to strengthen your eternalization of wholeness, of energy and of good eternal truth expressing. Become totally open to what we tell you here. To be whole is to obey the law of the God of the Universe. To be fully in command of your body is the way God intends. To be wholly operating within the law is what each master of greatness must strive to do.

To be a master requires a discipline, yes, but to enter into this study tells us that you want to hold a partnership with God at your center. Therefore, what better way to do this than to eternalize this partnership and bring your open mind into the work that must be done?

Bring the Pure Truth, the eternal truth, the "peterstet" truth into each decision. Team up with these truths that will put new energy into the earth, into your being, into those with whom you work. To be the master who can do all this, you must respond with alacrity to the understanding which is at the center of this chapter. That which is given you here is to put your understanding eternally open to what is eventually the only truth that will work in the earth plane.

Thinking of a previous chapter that suggested we are to work within our temples as if we are in a laboratory, I inserted three questions. "Are we to practice putting 'peterstet' truth into operation in the earth plane? Could we expect right now to get the perfect truth for each problem and to use that truth to solve it? Are we to abandon all 'teteract' truth?

The answer came immediately.

The questions all team up to ask, "Will God-mind truth produce the great results we promise?" We enter our assurance that what we tell you is true. Why hesitate? Eternalize our good help here in this plane and seek the "peterstet" truth daily to enact it NOW, not later when the New Age is completely upon you. Of course you must practice! Of course you must eternalize if you are to bring about the greatness we speak of.

Those who read this and think that we speak of something you will do later are not in syncopation with what is said here. Those who read into this chapter the thought that all we speak of is for the future and not now have entirely missed the point. Begin now, reader, begin now to work within your temple where the private laboratory resides. Team up with those who help you and ready yourself for a great adventure.

Go to your individual teachers and seek counsel on matters that bother you. The teacher will enter into your being and there the two of you will work through your questions to the perfect answers that you need to become a true master. Teamwork is the way to proceed, the way to bring understanding in the matters we speak of.

This chapter is not asking for your opinions. We team up, but we do not wait for your thoughts. We expect you to go to your teacher at whatever point you begin to think in "teteract" terms. That teacher, who is steeped in the way of the masters, will then bring you the open channel that you may gather the perfect truth that will pour through for you, the "peterstet" truth. With your own perfect truth plus the laws and the principles you will enter into the next phase of our work together.

Hold yourself open to even harder concepts, great thoughts that challenge your mind/spirit to its highest process. Those who work with you, your teachers, will not find vast concepts too difficult. They will know them because they use them regularly in all of their bright and happy lives. They will help you, too, to become one with these concepts, these understandings. Therefore, hold the thought that you are in the process of becoming, not the being who is already great beyond any help!

Now we turn to the next chapter that will open the truth even further, a chapter where we will call forth the masters to perform their truth.

The Teamwork of Truth

14

Am I ready for total commitment?

Much to my surprise, this chapter ended with only fifty lines on the word processor screen. I waited, but my fingers slid from the keys. This chapter, I was told, is a transition that allows the reader the opportunity to either team up with even greater commitment or to end the study with honor.

The message began.

The teamwork that brings the eternal good into manifestation now moves with the speed of light. The teamwork pushes toward its goal of putting the masters into the earth plane to right the wrongs that earth-mind has put there. It is not possible to overstate this matter, for today you must decide whether or not you will move into the second part of this study, the part that requires the total being, not a part time interest or a part time commitment.

Those of you who have made the total commitment will not be affected by what we say here. But those of you who hang on the fence between earth-mind and God-mind, between the decision to give full teamwork or not to enter into this teamwork, we say **today you must decide.**

Be of good cheer, for there is no condemnation toward those who cannot take the rest of the course. We who write these books through the writer, through the one we name Truth-giver, will not condemn you, nor will the God of the Universe condemn you. We only want, at this point, to arrest the half- committed ones and offer them a chance to retreat.

Those who are not suited to this work, those who are not given to the kind of hard work, the concentrated mind/spirit that is required to be a master of greatness are now given their freedom. To continue is to put yourself into our hands, into the hands of those teachers who strive with you to bring forth the Pure Truth of your being.

Those who retreat still have much of value to give to the earth. Their teamwork is important and will be used. But they will not be the masters. They will be those who point the way to the truth. Those who now feel they have come to the point where they must drop out remain open to our incoming truth. They open to the Pure Truth of their beings, and they present themselves to the teamwork of the New Age.

Those who stay, however, must now head toward the ultimate goal. Their goal is to thrust the valuable God-mind truth into the earth plane without a great time delay or with uncertainty. We now put you to further tests, to further experimentation. Team up, those who have remained as candidates to the master of greatness. Team up to demonstrate beyond what you thought possible, even for those who showed forth their perfection to the world — the one named Jesus, the one named Moses, the one named Isaiah, the one named Ethan. They showed forth greatness; yes, but you will now be called upon to be even more than they. Therefore, team up to begin.

Those who pour themselves into this study will generate great energy in the earth — the energy that will begin now to pour truth into the earth itself. The eternal teamwork now pours itself into the work at hand, into the eternalizations that will bring God power to bear upon all that is entered therein.

Promises that Become Gold

15

What must I learn to become a master of greatness?

Those who have recommitted themselves to the study are open to the thought that we who enter into their work will lead them into greatness. Those who now reinvest their time, their truth, their total energy toward becoming masters now stand forth to accept our plan for putting their truth into the earth plane with alacrity, with energy, with teamwork.

To open fully to the plan we present, turn now to your teacher who is ready to work with you.

The teacher assigned to me came in the instant that I opened my mind to the thought. "The teacher you want is here, Truth-giver," I heard within my mind. "I will help you through this study, through this eternal truth that will make you a true master." I waited, but apparently the teacher had no more to say at that time.

The Brotherhood continued with the chapter.

Eternalizations of your power, your oneness with all that is God now abound on this plane. Those who work with the study help those of us who write the chapter to put each of you into the teamwork of pure understanding. These special helpers hover near you and will assist your individual teachers to hold you in this eternalization that we have described. Your feeling nature may or may not recognize this work. We do not depend on emotions, remember.

Teamwork will bring your mind/spirit into its own precious understanding of who you are or what you are. Let this understanding spread throughout your being. You will now receive a name, a spirit name that will be used in the work. This name is yours only, yours to use and yours to hear when the occasion calls for it. The teachers will use these names because they designate the completely committed spirit, not the human entity with the body self. This step is important; it is truly "peterstet" truth.

Therefore, at this point enter into your temple and become perfectly quiet. Team up with the one who is your teacher to reassess the who or the what of you. Nothing must disturb this time you have together, and no other issue must be brought to your or the teacher's attention. Concentrate. Who or what are you? Go deeply within the temple and rest in whatever way you enjoy resting there. Invite the teacher. Concentrate on the teacher who will be your mirror, your reflection.

I went easily into my temple. I floated in a stream bounded with blue and yellow flowers. My teacher soon joined me, saying, "The one who is your teacher is here. Use me." We floated together until it seemed we became one. "What do you see?" a voice asked. "What eternalizes within you?"

Great light, not white, not glaring, just restful — that's what I saw. "What else?" said the voice. There was something there — far away, almost a pinpoint. "Could this be a goal?" the voice asked. The stream, with me in it, began to flow rapidly toward that pinpoint. I resisted. The stream moved even faster. Suddenly I looked into the colors of purple, pink and blue. What did this mean? "Enter the colors," said the voice. I pushed through the colors without fear. As the colors surrounded me, I wondered what I was supposed to learn.

"Gentle being," the voice said. "Heed my call and come forth to be what you are in reality." Was I that color combi-

nation, that vaporous something? "What you are is not body," came the voice.

"I AM spirit," I responded. But I already knew that. "Is this the lesson — that I AM spirit?" No answer. When I thought "move" my spirit moved. I experimented. "Go to the beautiful ocean where I love to be." No response. "I see the ocean." I thought again, and the green ocean swirled in a giant circle with me in it. "I see the great canyon on Kauai." By the time the thought went out, I glided into that deep expanse and floated toward the red and black walls that bounded the canyon. I was examining the walls at close range when I suddenly became one with them! Yes, I was, as far as I could determine, part of the substance.

"The truth opens to you. Be what you are," came the voice.

I thought of my daughter in Italy. There I was within her seeing what she saw, gently performing the loving mother tasks with her little son. Startled, I quickly withdrew.

The being that I AM is not separate from matter or people. I AM somehow part of the entire scope of being. Is this what I was to learn?

"The tender truth washes over you, Truth-giver," said my teacher. "Though you always have thought you are spirit, this time you have experienced spirit. There is a difference."

I kept notes throughout the adventure. My experience is not meant to be **your** *guide,* **your** *truth or* **your** *understanding. I merely give you what is memorable and significant to the mind/spirit the Brotherhood calls "Truth-giver."*

Now the message from the Brotherhood continued.

Those who have experienced their own truth, as this writer has, are ready to proceed. There is no way to bring you total understanding all at once. We must proceed step by step in the manner we are now doing. Therefore, open yourself for another truth, another promise of greatness.

Reach out with your spirit, whom you now recognize, to gain the view of the earth you live upon. Team up with your teacher yet again in the temple of your being where you work with this material. Know now the rapidity with which you have reached the spirit, the inner reality of you. Bring this which you are into focus. Team up with this reality in order to use it.

There! The spirit self of you emerges. This self knows the open truth — that it is your perfect reality, that it is the part that has true value. Therefore, it waits quietly to see what is next, for it recognizes that you are now engaged in work that will make it stronger.

Bring this spirit self of you with its own colors into focus. Those colors brighten, they enter one another, blend, then separate, then blend again. This engagement of colors eternalizes as the reality which is aware of its worth, its entering goodness and its perfect truth incoming.

The "peterstet" truth is now ready to unfold. This truth now enters to help you give yourself yet another eternal truth of God's wonderful promises regarding those he works with. The only way to truly understand the many promises that God gives you is to experience them for yourself. In other books we have listed promises, but only your intellectual self dealt with them. Now your reality must deal with them.

Put your "peterstet" truth to work on the matter of God's great goodness. By opening your spirit to goodness, you will enter into the goodness as the writer entered into the walls of the canyon. The goodness that we hold up here is that which God enters into the earth. When you know what this goodness is, you will place great value upon it and use it with generous abandon to help reinstate truth into this earth.

Now work with your teachers, candidates for greatness. Eternalize the temple of your being and go there now. Enter and allow time to prepare for your teacher.

My inner temple holds many possibilities for restful meditation. I did not go to the stream as I did the first time. Instead, I floated upwards to a high dome. Below this dome is a window that overlooks a much loved scene on the Florida coast. From there I can watch gray and white porpoises rise magnificently from the sea into the clear air in a triumphant, exhilarating show. To one side is a blue and white sailboat, and beyond that scene, the sun glimmers in golden promise on the horizon. Waves push toward the shore and fall on the soft, fine sand in light bursts of white foam.

"Now is the time, Truth-giver," came my teacher's message. "The student must open to the teacher to learn more about this place you like so much." I was again that color combination of purple, pink and blue — my spirit self.

"Be what you know you are — perfect spirit." I mused on those words. "The God of the Universe has something to enter into your being! Be alert." My vaporous self teamed up with the words and waited.

"There!" came an announcement. I peered out the window. But I was no longer in the temple! I was beside the huge porpoises who continued their jumping and diving. Those wonderful sleek animals eyed me now and then, but they were not concerned about my presence. Abruptly I became part of the largest porpoise who dived deep into the sparkling ocean, turned and rose quickly to burst to the surface and into the sunshine. When the porpoise and I fell back into the water with an enormous splash, I drifted away and became, I finally decided, part of the water. I wanted to rise above the ocean as myself, but instead, I returned to my inner temple.

"The truth, Truth-giver?" the teacher's voice asked. "What is the truth?"

"The I AM of me, that vaporous purple, pink and blue, is not limited as to its substance or form. Is that it?"

A moment's hesitation, and my teacher said, "The wonderful truth applies here that you in your reality have the potential to belong to the earth substance, to move it about, to become it."

Though fascinating, my superficial assessment of what I learned didn't seem to have practical value. What did it matter that I could soar out to be one with a porpoise, one with the ocean?

"Now try again," said the teacher.

Without great enthusiasm I again stood at the window of my temple and soared forth. This time I knew I was a pinpoint of something that existed. This time I pushed beyond the point where the porpoises carried on their morning frolic. I became the traveler on her way to some distant point, as yet unknown.

Energy circled around me lifting me higher and higher, and I could see a white cumulus cloud in the making. Finally, it became a giant towering cloud that sailed majestically with me riding upon it. This cloud grew in volume and grew in energy. Within it there was lightning, not angry or fearful lightning, but the kind of light that brightened the entire cloud and then subsided.

I rode that cloud across the Florida peninsula to the Gulf of Mexico where I disengaged myself to drop gracefully away from the cloud and down into the beautiful sparkling ocean where I descended to the sand and mud that lay on the deep bottom. Gray-green plants, lighted only by a dim glow, waved slowly in rhythm with the movement of the water. Great pale fish swam about seeking a food supply among the plants.

I felt uncomfortable on this journey, and I ended it.

"The experience speaks to you, Truth-giver. Hear the truth." The truth? I — my reality — have no limitations. Is this it? "Gently, Truth-giver. Enter into study on this. Become one with the great truth, not the first truth that comes to mind!" But the greater truth eluded me.

"The greater truth must unfold to you by experience, not by my explanation," my teacher responded.

The chapter then continued.

The writer's experience must be gone through again, must enter her into more experiences before she learns the truth that is hers to learn. Remember, the lessons to be learned are not always the same for all. The experience that each of you teamed up with in the beginning was similar in that you became spirit. Then when you returned to that spirit form, the lessons to learn depended upon your own inner growth. The writer's lesson is not the same as yours. Yours is not similar to another's. There is no higher or less high lesson here. There are only lessons that teach growth, understanding and partnership with the God of the Universe.

The promises that unfold as you put yourself into spirit form and let your teacher lead you are those that your own spirit is seeking. Therefore, we cannot enter the promises in alphabetical order! The promises that unfold to each of you are the questions that the very mind/spirit of you asks and seeks to find answers for. They are the golden thoughts that penetrate into your being and go forth into the earth plane as the substance that enriches the earth, teams up with the eternal truth and gives people what they need and long for in their lives. Yes, these promises that your soul eternalizes will be the coin of the realm that produces what you must produce in order to bring good into the New Age.

Postscript

The chapter ended, but I had not learned my lesson. I asked to try again.

"The open teamwork between us, Truth-giver, is that we have teamed up to bring the lesson into better understanding. That you have not recognized this lesson is the marvel. What do you now give to the experience that you missed before? Think on the answer."

I had already reread the second experience and had given it much thought. One thing I learned is that when one is reluctant to participate, nothing is positive. I had felt that the entire adventure was thrust upon me, though I don't think it was. Perhaps I didn't like what happened to me because I seemed to have no control.

"The truth is that you wanted to be released to pursue your own thoughts! You did not want to receive lessons! The openness with which we work reveals your poor thoughts to me. To enable you to get the truth that you must understand, I will outline what happened.

"The truth that will not penetrate you is that you stopped the greatness by turning your mind to negative thoughts. The greatness which was on its way to performing within you gave way to your being who wanted to turn toward other thoughts, other ideas."

Should I leave this postscript in? I debated with myself. It was far from flattering!

"The truth, that is the question to get answered!" my teacher announced.

Why was I so dense? What had I done wrong — or left undone?

Several hours later I quieted my mind, and I abandoned negative self-criticism in favor of positive action. I made my God-mind connection and then received these words: "You are not to master truth alone, Truth-giver! Team up! Your being wants help, wants surfeit, wants consciousness of My Presence, My Sustenance. It does not want to be out on these assignments alone. Now do you understand? My Being is your Partner."

How could I have missed the basic truth of the partnership with the God of the Universe? My teacher said, "That which is now understood must be used. To enter into the experience is to make it yours forever. To write it down is only to write it down.

"Team up! The new experience is now underway, the one you will better enjoy."

Again I went into my temple where I stood at the open window overlooking the Atlantic Ocean off the Florida coast. My thoughts centered on my spirit, that which I have seen as purple, pink and blue. I stood at my temple window knowing I was not alone, that my Teammate/Partner — the God of the Universe — would go with me.

This time we soared upward, and the porpoises became tiny dots. The ocean became more blue than green as we rose higher and higher. Finally I did not look toward earth, only outward toward an unknown destination. I began to wonder if I should take some control. I asked, "What does a candidate for master of greatness need to know?"

No answer, but a change in direction soon showed me that we were heading back toward earth. We entered a huge towering cloud that was approaching the shoreline at Floridana Beach. We penetrated the cloud and began to work with it, flattening it out, pressing it down until it hung near the earth and began to shower raindrops. People on the beach were surprised, and I saw them laugh. Some opened their mouths to receive the fresh rain water. The cloud then went across the peninsula in that same form presenting showers along the way.

I was within that cloud as I was before, but this time there was power and understanding of how to make use of that cloud to benefit the earth. Again we went to Kauai and together soared through the canyon. Again I went into the walls, but this time I did not look out blankly. I listened! I heard, finally, the faint rhythmic beat of the earth itself, its own creativity at work, its spirit that works to bring good to that which is matter.

What a different experience! I was not afraid; I was not uneasy. I was not alone.

Teamwork — the Stream of Gold

16

What am I to learn about my partnership with God?

The Brotherhood believes that an honest revelation of my ups and downs in accomplishing this lesson will help other candidates who may be having a difficult time of it. I kept notes on my struggle to understand the power of teamwork, and later I wove them into the fabric of the chapter itself. Therefore, they are yours to read, yours to study, yours to use in any way that might help.

The Brotherhood began with more explanations of the power of teamwork.

To open fully to our teamwork, you must enter into the eternalization that we now outline to you. This eternalization will help you move into the teamwork quickly and with authority, not hesitantly and with vague hope. Therefore, we now encourage your full participation in order to wrest your truth into the eternalization and thus into the earth plane.

The way to eternalize is to put your truth into picture form. That means that your truth, whatever it is, must translate itself into open recognition on the earth plane. To understand this work, hold onto the thought and enter into our example. Some person, perhaps you, wants to provide much food to feed the hungry.

Those who mill about with fear, anger and hopelessness see you as their hope. To meet this situation, hold the truth that enters, that which God-mind provides, into picture form.

The truth may be, for example, that God is the Supplier of all needed good. To translate this truth into earth form, think of the great supply of edible matter that will nourish many bodies, no matter how many eat. To eternalize this truth, picture the people eating from the teamwork that you, the Partner, God, and those advanced spirits on this plane work together to bring about. The eternalization must be yours because you know the need; you also know the way to bring satisfaction to those who eat. Besides, you are the earth form who can help them to focus on the supply.

Therefore, when you hear the need, eternalize the truth that comes to you into the earth products that will serve the needs of the multitude. That is your part. Then you enter into the teamwork — by teaming up in spirit — with the Teammate and with the Brothers who know how to help.

I had a question. "Is this method the one Jesus used to feed the multitude?" (Matthew 15: 32-38)

Jesus opened himself fully to the truth that came to him through the open channel, the Pure Truth that came to him from God-mind. Then he acted upon that truth. This Brother of Brothers perfectly illustrates how each person in his lifetime experience may put truth to work. Therefore, look not to Jesus as the entering God who performed miracles, but as the Brother who showed those around him how they could live their lives.

To wrest the truth into the earth plane, you must hold no earth-mind truth. To perform a seeming miracle, you must free yourself from any limiting thought that will obstruct the eternalization that will perform its truth in the visible earth plane. These eternal truths that we share with you must ring true within you, they must ring the bell of recognition as to what is perfect and understandable.

Now we team up with you to bring you the way you, too, can perform a miracle. Team up with your teacher at this point. Then eternalize the one truth that enters through the open channel from God-mind. Team up with whatever truth is there, not giving way to doubt, to uncertainty, to belief in earth-mind truth over God-mind truth.

As an aside to me, You, the perfect Truth-giver, will perform the very thing we speak of here. Now enter into your temple with your teacher, and proceed in your next experiment.

I entered into my temple and found two golden chairs. I sat down in one and my teacher sat in the other. My teacher began.

"Now the teamwork begins. That which now enters you is my own truth that I understand and can help you to perform in the earth plane. Therefore, team up with it. This truth is that every good that enters the earth plane starts with an eternalization from one who is in the earth plane. This understanding means that you, the one in human form, can begin any process of greatness that you want to start."

My thoughts churned this way and that, but I made no decision. After a few moments, I asked my teacher about getting my own God-mind truth before I began. (In retrospect I see my usual hesitation in the face of greatness.)

"The entering truth eternalizes within you already. What is it?" my teacher asked.

And from my own God-mind connection came my truth.

"Gentle beings approach. They enter to help you to manifest the truth that I AM the wonderful Partner, the One Who helps bring your truth into manifestation."

My mind drew a blank. The words were clear enough, but I had expected something different. From the advantage of hindsight, I wonder why I didn't concentrate on the message I received. Obviously it was my key.

The window of my study was open, and I heard the bird songs that, in varied tones and rhythms, spoke about their lives. What were their needs? I tried to enter into the earth to listen to its message. Obviously, I was getting nowhere.

"What are you going to do?" my teacher asked.

"I don't really know yet," I replied.

"Then team up with me to search for your answer." Relieved, I accepted this idea.

"That which is now yours may be put into the earth. The promise you have received is that your Partner helps you to bring truth into manifestation."

But I already knew that! Why was my teacher repeating what I had already received?

"Then make use of this partnership."

Thinking I had a blank check of sorts, I decided that the need was rain. I looked at the sky. No clouds were visible. But the earth needed rain, I reasoned. The birds, too, needed rain to drink, to help grow their food, to provide for their entire well being. Neither the earth nor the birds told me these things. They were my conclusions. Though I was to bring my truth into manifestation, I persistently ignored it. My ego determined everything — the needs and the solutions. Not once did I include my Partner.

Turning to my teacher, I waited for advice.

"That which is yours to give is yours to eternalize."

At the time, the answer seemed ambiguous. I turned to this teacher again and waited for more explanation.

"That which you decide to bring forth, enact with the power of your Partner Who now wants you to use the partnership openly."

I eternalized — projected — the picture of gentle rain falling on the world around me. The picture clarified into the sound, the smell, the sight of rain that opened the ground, nourished the plants, held itself to the task of renewal, not destruction.

My Partner, the Voice of Truth, entered my meditation.

"Be still; enter into My Being. Together we will enter into the process to bring rain or whatever you think is needed. Team up with My understanding, My energy, My perfection."

But I did not wait to include my Partner's greatness. I merely took those words at their superficial value and thought, "Now I am part of the creative process."

"Release your energy into the Pure Truth here.Release your understanding, your eternalization which soars to the destination. Watch it perform!"

I waited. I ate lunch. I waited some more. No clouds formed. What was wrong?

"That which eternalizes within you is not eternalized to express truth, it is eternalized to express rain! When you want to demonstrate truth, think 'truth,' not the object you intend to enter the earth plane!"

Wasn't I to project that which I wanted to enter the earth plane, that which would meet a need? Impatience gnawed at me.

"Be still. Team up with each thought that now is brought to your mind. Think. Be quiet. Team up. The projection or eternalization is that which you know to be the truth. What is your truth?"

By this time I was so confused I had to review the chapter to find it. My truth: that my Partner is the One Who helps me bring truth into manifestation. I reread it several times. I interpreted it. This promise means that I do not have to depend on myself to accomplish greatness, for surely I could not project truth on my own. Therefore, I can and must depend fully on the Partner.

"Then team up and enter into that partnership, Truth-giver!"

I felt at that moment much as I felt when I first tried to team up with the Brotherhood of God. There were doubts then, and there were doubts again. I wrote, "I depend on the Partner, and I can speak of this partnership and write of it. But now that the time has come to put this partnership to the test, I am weak kneed and hesitant. What if I fail? What if God fails?"

A faint stirring, a nudge within my spirit/mind, and my teacher responded to my questions.

"What teams up with you, Truth-giver, is that earth truth is making its assault upon your God-mind truth! Eternalize the entering God truth that you may thwart this entity that sneaks up on you to undermine your truth in progress."

This ***entity?*** *What was meant by* ***entity?***

"We mean the earth-mind truth that holds you in its vise-like grip, that pours every known obstacle onto the situation, that offers you pure doubt, pure emptiness! That is why we use the word ***entity.*** *This insidious truth works much like an entity who would physically restrain your body."*

Discouraged, I wondered why I was pursuing this study which leads to a master of greatness.

"That which passes through your mind is now leaving it."

My teacher said this with some humor. No, I cannot say exactly why I know humor was present. Perhaps I felt it.

"Eternalize the partnership, and hold it within you."

My teacher pressed me to continue. I tried.

"Put your Partner into place as the One with power, the One who has that which gives impetus to spirit, to substance, too. This Partner knows your hesitation, but does not call you 'weak.' He only patiently waits to work with you. Think on this."

Self-condemning thoughts pierced my being.

"Never think yourself unworthy, Truth-giver, or you only compound the problem. The thought that you wrestle with is helping you to get the right ideas. Now team up with this thought and let it lead you. ***Do not think to lead it.*** *This understanding is important, for if you try to lead the thought that God is Partner and that His truth is all that matters, you force the issue instead of letting the thought grow. Enter into the idea of growth, not of banging this thought into your being as a carpenter would hammer a nail!"*

With this last colorful illustration, I decided to leave the matter overnight. When I returned to the chapter, I asked if I should leave out the story of my own struggle with truth. The answer from the Brotherhood, who helps me to channel this material from God-mind, was that the reader may also experience some of what I was going through.

The Brotherhood then told me to return to the chapter and work it through.

That which now bothers you must find answers, even as the reader must find answers. Team up with your teacher yet again. This process, and it is an entirely new process to you, must be gone through successfully if you are to go on with the study. Then when you have teamed up with your teacher, tenderly assess your thoughts, your goal, your entire outlook in the matter of demonstration.

I again went to my temple, and for awhile I wanted to be there alone to think. This temple came into being because the Brotherhood wanted me to learn truth that would help me to grow. Those who came here to work with me, to help me to brighten and decorate this temple did so with great personal understanding of my nature. I was unwilling to have an ornate temple because deep inside I did not feel worthy of such grandeur. I could not fathom a God who wanted me to have beauty in my life just for the sake of beauty. Perhaps some of those old feelings about unworthiness, about God being high on a throne and unreachable, unconcerned, were still thwarting my growth.

Through my own God-mind connection, I again received assurances of my worth, of my value to the God of the Universe. Along with these assurances, I was told that our partnership — God's and mine — is not a sometime thing. It is for all the time. It isn't for later; it is for now. The partnership is mine, not with uncertainty, but with powerful certainty.

Again, my teacher addressed me.

"Now, Truth-giver, team up with my reason for working with you. This relationship is to welcome you into a new understanding which must be yours."

So, where do I begin?

"To enter into perfect understanding, you must repeat the laws and the principles we have taught already. Remember those? Remember the principles of God's goodness, His entering power, His energy which reaches out to be used by those who open themselves to it? Well, review these in your mind."

I did so. God is more than Being, more than any concept I can bring forth, but it is important to have some idea of what God IS. These laws and principles, for example, are there to be used by anyone who is audacious enough to reach out to make use of them. Was I not audacious enough? Was that my problem?

In chapter 3, "The Brotherhood of God and You," I reviewed what was said concerning using goodness as the ma-

terial expression of truth. An example was given of a person who wants to be a master of greatness in the New Age. He chooses a speciality — shelter. Then the entering goodness is explained as being that actual shelter in the earth plane. The truth back of this demonstration is not that shelter is a good thing to have, but that the teamwork brings it about.

What this means to me, then, is that I see a need and I salute this need as one that can be met. I see dry ground and plants rising from the earth and looking wilted. The earth, apparently, needs rain — gentle, non-threatening steady rain. I present this need to my Brothers, and I say, "What do you think of this eternalization?" Then, if there is agreement in this eternalization of rain, we (the Brothers and I) take the eternalization to the God of the Universe, the Source of all good.

My thoughts ran along the following lines. Does my eternalization meet the test? Is it for the general good of the earth and mankind? Yes, it does seem that it is. Will it produce that which is worthy of perfect tenderness? Yes, it appears worthy. I asked the Brothers, "Can this eternalization of a gentle rainfall to renew the earth in this community be consideredworthy?"

Those who come with alacrity in all matters responded.

"The rainfall is not eternal truth. The eternal truth here is that the earth is now in its recreative period, now entered in an overall renewing of its resources. To present rain is to eternalize what is (already) entered in the earth by the God of the Universe."

I still did not understand the lesson. My teacher continued.

"The rain of your eternalization is not the right thing to concentrate on, Truth-giver. Team up with the earth itself, the very nature of the earth. Enter into it and eternalize what you learn there."

The I AM of myself, the purple, pink and blue spirit self, disengaged itself to sink right through our house and into the ground. There I waited, listening.

"No need of the earth can be met by making rain. Team up with our true needs, our wending truth here in that which

comprises the soil and the underworld of growth. Hear the wending need that tenders itself to your listening ear."

I opened myself as fully as I could to the sounds of each plant that wound its way through the earth bound on its own mission. Was it a sighing I heard? Or was it a deep grating and rasping breath? What was the message?

"My plants need more than rain. They need the purity of every gentle drop of moisture." Was this a thought coming from the earth itself? "They want the precious oxygen, the hydrogen, the wrested minerals of the earth substance to clarify themselves. What can you do to bring this clarity, this purity?"

Frankly, I didn't know. I withdrew from the earth with greater insight. No, rain was not the immediate problem at all. The atmosphere above and within the earth needed repair. But what can I do?

Then I realized I had let my spirit go on a mission all on its own, without my Partner. I had gone to learn, but again I had forgotten the One with power. Finally, I teamed up consciously with my Partner, and Light infused my purple, pink and blue self. This time we reentered the earth together.

We did not stay in the ground beneath my house. We traveled deep into the earth, deep into its hot center which seemed quite small. The earth was not the active thing I had expected. There were bubbles rising from the interior of the earth — red, molten bubbles. The problem was, I understood, that there were too few of these bubbles going upward from its center. The core was not activating them in the abundance that the earth needed. Were these bubbles — large teardrops of red-orange — the renewal of the earth substance? Was this the recreative process at work within the planet? Why were there so few bubbles? What could motivate this core to produce more? What was the problem? What could I do about the problem?

The Partner and I rose from the ground into the sunshine, into the cool air that seemed pure and wholesome. The Partner held me to Him, and took me high into the atmosphere, higher and higher until I could see the world below. But it was enveloped in a soupy or murky cloud of some kind.

"Be My gentle Truth-giver. Tell what you have seen and tell it without fear of those who would ridicule."

And so I have told the story. My specialization is presenting truth, and my truth — that "I AM the wonderful Partner, the One Who helps bring your truth into manifestation" — is now demonstrated. How? I learned that when I work alone, I am teamed up with earth-mind truth, and I work with the tools of indecision and thwarted efforts. But when I turn to God-mind, I turn to the power that God IS.

"You received a true revelation, Truth-giver — the truth of the planet. Had you produced rain, the earth would have been poorly served. That which you were to point out has been accomplished."

Perhaps, among the readers, there are some who tenderly team up with the Partner and then produce rain. There will be others who produce shelter or food supplies.

The Brotherhood then offered the following.

That which the writer has learned is how to manifest her own truth. But unless you team up to enter your truth to the earth plane, you will have gone amiss. Her experience is only hers, not yours. Her truth enters as it was eternalized, not as you may eternalize. Therefore, know only that the writer's goals and your goals are not the same, and only your teachers can help you attain what is yours to attain.

Bright Teamwork Puts You into the Flow

17

How can I project and manifest something specific?

To manifest the truth of God into earth substance, join the teamwork of the Brotherhood and the Partner Who unites His power with you. To be the master of greatness who manifests God truth, which will suffice as the good that people want and need, never overlook the potential to be achieved through teamwork. You are the prime mover, the one who opens your mind to teamwork. Without teamwork, you merely stand on the earth with great visions that never team up with earth material.

Team up with this understanding — that **teamwork produces the great truth into substance,** not the one who you are, the master who opens to our good truth. The one who only teams up with himself in the earth plane relies on earth-mind truth which calls forth the need of hard work and turmoil.

"Team up" was the first instruction I received from the Brotherhood. Without teamwork, there would be no books. Was this message any different?

That which we now emphasize is not quite the same. The way to greatness is the entering truth that offers you its wisdom, its energy, its perfection. To use the gifts that open to you, use teamwork all the way. Absorbing thoughts is one kind of teamwork, but to put the thoughts into the substance that those in the earth plane can use, is another.

Therefore, the first explanation was about the teamwork that helped you to communicate with us (the Brotherhood). Then the God-mind connection was introduced, and now the Pure Truth comes to you, and you must now enact it into the earth plane. How will this come about? Why, by becoming one with the entire teamwork concept, not just part of it.

To manifest goodness, you must team up with that which we lay out before you, that which we urge you to use, to put into motion. The writer thinks that the difficulty lies in the newness of this concept. But this concept is **not** new, candidates. The concept is old. Mankind turned away from the teamwork to work with their hands, their feet and their brains, and greatness ebbed away.

The easy way is the God-truth way. The hard way is the earth-truth method. Bring yourself into right thinking, right understanding, and you will form eternalizations that will project easily into the earth plane. Remember, manifestation is accomplished with teamwork, not by yourself. Teamwork is the God-truth way. The way to poverty and lack, the way to illness and poor health, the way to hopelessness and despair is the way of earth-mind truth.

To bring your Pure Truth into manifestation, you must think "truth," not an object or a condition you want to bring about. The writer proved this point in Chapter 16. To bring truth into manifestation — this is the goal the master must enter into, not the eternalization of the object or the condition. The writer kept trying to eternalize rain, which her community needed. That she might understand what she was doing wrong, we let her continue to eternalize until she saw for herself that nothing happened. She wondered why, and at this point she opened her mind that we might help her to understand.

Therefore, to help the candidates for master of greatness get into the eternalization that will bring them into truth processed into the earth, we will now proceed. To wrest the eternalization into the earth plane, put it into the partnership of the One Who is your gentle Teammate or Partner. Those in the Brotherhood will help you to form the eternalization that it may truly be in line with truth, but the One Who will project it into the earth plane is the God of the Universe, not the Brotherhood.

Let us review. What is your speciality? What will you be responsible for doing in the New Age? Do you have this in mind? If not, review that part of the book. Then, when you know for sure what your speciality is, leap to share it with the Brotherhood. They will enter your temple to see that which you have brought forth. They will, if you ask, give you their opinions, but not as they are given on the earth plane, candidates. These opinions come from advanced spirits who believe in your open mind, your teamwork, your greatness that will manifest in the earth.

What you want to produce is teamed up with earth material when you adhere to the procedure we present. The only way to be successful is to use the power of God, the energy of greatness. To ignite your eternalization on your own is very difficult. Unless you fully understand and make use of the process, the thought projection will wilt where it stands, fade to nothingness and remain within, never to be seen in the outer earth plane.

Now, let us go into the laboratory where you work with truth. We enter there with you this time because we eternalize you as one who is ready to use the process. The perfection of your beautiful thought projection must now be entered into this laboratory.

Stopping the flow of instructions, I asked what kind of thing we were to project?

Those who remain teamed up with us will now receive instructions. Bring into this laboratory the idea of true beauty, true loveliness. That which you focus on is now entered. Team up! Be assured that these pictures you have entered — all pictures of beauty of some kind — must now eternalize into bright teamwork.

At the time of this writing, spring insistently beckoned me and other Missourians outdoors. Warm, gentle breezes whispered to me about my duties to the soil, to the plants and to the migrating birds. It was time to gather my resources, spiritual and physical, and prepare my flower bed and planters for this year's flower selection.

Therefore, I chose flowers as the true loveliness that I wished to bring into earth form. "Pull our resources into the picture you hold," the inner voice suggested, and I reached out with my mind/spirit to touch the creative energy that worked within nature. "Use what is now expressed to prepare the soil," continued the voice.

Step by step I received instructions from an intelligence outside myself in this preparation. I was to use the mulch in the back section of our property and mix it with other soil from the flower bed and from the planters. Now this mulch held no particular attributes that either my husband or I knew about. Actually, it consisted of grass clippings and dog manure. (I can see long-time mulch gardeners wincing.)

I questioned the spiritual wisdom that understood about soil. "When I was in a garden club, I was told that dog manure is not good for plants."

The Brotherhood's response was firm.

Use the manure and the mulch content that is the oldest and the most blended. Stir it all up and mix with the soil. That which you do will bring precious properties into the soil.

With a mental shrug, I placed the plan into my inner laboratory, into the place where teamwork takes hold to refine and to present even greater thoughts.

We who now work with you, we who ride the winds that caress the land, we who want the central message understood, team up with you in this work.

With no small amount of excitement, I entered wholeheartedly into the plan. Those who sustained me in this effort were always at hand to advise, to encourage, to give me needed physical energy. Every bucket of mulch I raised over the fence and emptied into our garden cart held a promise of partnership with that aspect of God we name nature.

Eventually the half barrel on the back patio was prepared, and I filled it with periwinkle plants. Each large pot received the same mulch mixture. I put asparagus ferns in the largest pot and red geranimum plants into the other two pots. The front flower bed also received an ample mixture of mulch, and I planted salvia — scarlet sage — for the hummingbirds and put in a border of blue ageratums. Since my wood planter box was mostly in shade, impatiens were the obvious choice there.

"Well, it's done," I said. Almost immediately a message came to me from my teacher.

"Watch. Watch the teamwork take hold."

I wondered, however briefly, how I would react if the plants died in this mixture of mulch so different from the sterile bagged dirt we usually bought and mixed with commercial fertilizers. But the word given me was "watch." So I watched.

The periwinkles, a long time favorite of mine, did nothing interesting to the eye for several days. In fact, I had to prop the droopy little plants into an upright position at least twice a day!

"The action is in the roots," I was told.

For several days, the other plants stayed much as they were when I first planted them. Would they develop? Would they take to this mixture of unusual mulch? Many little weeds came up, something I never saw when I used the sterile dirt. There was activity there, all right, but none of it seemed apparent in the flowers.

"Watch," my teacher had told me. So I watched — two to three times a day. The impatiens were the first plants to show activity by sending out an abundance of new leaves. Each time I looked, I saw explosive evidence of new growth. A few pink blossoms soon appeared, then more and more until a mass of green and pink filled the planter box. Tiny hummingbirds and bumble bees spent considerable time probing the blooms. Meanwhile, the pale green periwinkle plants in the whiskey barrel stood erect and slowly deepened their color into a glossy, dark green. Their leaves thickened and the

plants sent out new stems with more glossy dark green leaves. My watchfulness was finally rewarded with a burst of violet periwinkle blossoms that waved toward the sun and never faded.

I spoke to the plants, tenderly expressing my appreciation. It seemed the natural thing to do under the circumstances. Again, my teacher reminded me.

"The plants heed the teamwork of you, those who undertake the encouragement of all plant life, and the Purity which is, of course, God."

"Watch," I heard from within my inner laboratory. I learned that the soil in the pots and flower bed stayed moist and cool throughout the hot days, and the plants did not wither or droop. There were other observations hard to explain in words. How do I express that sense of energy I perceived in the soil? What words do I use to tell you that there is communication — visible and invisable — within the plant bed and between gardeners and their plants?

Could it be, I wondered, that I was learning how to be one with what IS, one with all life that expresses both in spirit and in material form?

The Brotherhood answered my thoughts.

Those who work in the laboratory of Mind, those who enter into the projection of thought that teams up with what the very earth responds to, will generate the Will of the God of the Universe. That Will is, of course, the perfection of the earth, the purity of the planet, and the gathering of inner resources to take you to the tender outreach of Truth itself.

What the writer has opened to may or may not be what the reader opens to. Each spirit/mind teams up differently. Each spirit/mind expresses whatever it is that reflects the growth plan of that individual. Therefore, those who read of the writer's experiment may team up with what she has learned or they may not. The point here is not to display before you the writer's magnificence, but her own hesitancy, her doubts, her understanding which is enriched. To work within the laboratory is to use the resources at hand, the resources that will take the new master of greatness into whatever endeavor he or she must enter.

The writer brought great partnership into this account. To unite with the teamwork, each one must open his mind, his heart and be willing to exercise the partnership in regard to whatever is needed or required. We work with the reader and the writer to bring you all into the understanding that potential begins and ends only in the generous teamwork of divine partnership. To withstand the onslaughts of turmoil, to weather the storms which beset a lifetime experience, unite within the partnership. To wrest the value of the resources (of God) into the open and acknowledged earth plane, use what is yours — the truth that shatters all partnership with earth-mind. That which manifests will be noted by all and then acknowledged to be the pure and unbounded teamwork of that which is of God.

That which you now understand to be our teamwork — the Brotherhood and your teacher, the Partner who brings His power and perfection to your work — is the optimum energy at work in your life.

Persistent needs must be taken to your teacher. Each person is eternalized to bring forth the potential of each spirit/mind. Therefore, know you are not without help. Be encouraged to know that growth is a step by step matter, not the eternal truth that you would like to spring forth fully assimilated and put to work. That Which IS teams up with the perfect partnership between you and the God of the Universe. You no longer walk into the world to eternalize good by yourself. The teamwork is with you, the bright and gentle teamwork that eternalizes along with you to produce into the earth the reality of God truth.

This is the end of the chapter eternalized within the teamwork of the writer, the Brotherhood/teacher and the God of the Universe.

The Graduation Chapter 18

How will graduation affect my life?

When I graduated, along with twenty-three other students, from my rural Indiana high school, many adults passed along their best advice and philosophy. My parents pointed the way to college. Teachers counseled all seniors who were going after jobs or joining the military forces. And the speakers — baccalaureate, commencement — tried to join the past to the present, giving us the best wisdom they had.

College was more of a scholastic celebration. Honor students were recognized, degrees were conferred and tassels were moved from one side of our caps to the other. Parents, friends and fellow graduates celebrated together.

However, the conferring of master of greatness degrees, the graduation all candidates have been waiting for, is only vaguely like high school or college commencement. First, each candidate stands alone — except for the Brotherhood and the Partner. We cannot turn to one another to note the pleasure, the awe or wonderment the ceremony brings. Second, the role of a master of greatness is defined, lest we think amiss. Also, the course of study we have undertaken is reviewed and distilled that we may know for certain who we are.

We leave our status as candidates, and we become masters who unite with our Partner. It is this complete and absolute partnership which sets us apart as masters.

Here is what the Brotherhood told me.

You who become masters hold no individual thought of greatness manifested. Masters team up with their Partners, team up with the truth of the universe. You enter the world as those who have new tenderness, new understanding, new observations to put into the world.

When the partnership takes its rightful place in the center of your mind, where every thought rises from that alliance and not through your own ego, then your position as a master will become more obvious, not only to you, but to others as well. We enter this piece of advice. Say nothing to others, but enter into the partnership fully. They who want to know why your life is suddenly more tender, more joyful, more powerful, will seek the answer, and you can tell each person who asks. But make no pronouncements, no judgments, no great statements of power. That which is your perfection, the partnership, operates quietly, not with a battering ram.

The partnership must be reckoned with in the following manner. First, you are not a single mind operating within the earth structure. You are now the partnership that operates within the God-mind structure of Pure Truth. There is no more "I" in your life. The way to phrase what you are is "We." **The operating concept here is that you, the individualized spirit, operate as the expression of God.**

Second, your thinking is no longer that of an individual who operates his lifetime to boost himself. The new way is that you, the individual mind, now walks with the Partner Who has the perfect Mind, the powerful Mind, the optimum energy with which to bring truth into being. When you think of this teamwork, think of "tenderness," rather than of a binding agreement. To feel bound is not to be free, and this partnership is free.

Third, the truth of your God-mind connection is ready to be instated into the earth. This truth enters your mind openly, not through closed doors. Therefore, open your mind to that which is your Partner. Be joined in perfect association with your Partner who relays to your mind all it wants and needs. To strive toward goals you set is to thwart the eternalization. The partnership works with the ease of a well-oiled hinge. There it is, at the touch, not to be sorted out or to be wrestled with. Therefore, think of the partnership as a generous greatness that is now entered into your life. There it is to draw forth, to put into earth life, to use as the wonderful teamwork eternalizes. Rest in this assurance of wealth, for to become anxious is to slow the flow, to resist the incoming energy, to become less than the perfect half of the God partnership.

Be teamed up with the totality of the partnership, for to hold back your own consummation of it is to bring only generosity without power. This would mean that you would open to God as the Source, but you would not turn to Him as the powerful Presence that will instate truth within the earth. The totality is what any partnership must have if it is to become perfect. To understand this idea, we point out that the earth could not exist without the sun. This partnership has become total, has it not? What would the earth be without sunlight? The truth involved in this analogy is that God is the center, the optimum energy that activates that truth. The earth, you, teams up to bring forth the positive thrust of energy. Then the powerful alliance is obvious, for it functions perfectly.

The eternalization of your lifetime experience is what you, the spirit form, took to earth with you. The plan you hold within you is that the perfect alliance will bring your life into remarkable fruition. That is the way it works. The earth truth, however, has become so strong, so entered into the minds of mankind that it turns that bright plan into aberrations. That which began as brightness often ends in darkness. That which began in God often ends in despair.

To release yourselves, and others, from this earth truth pattern, you must enter into the partnership with the God of the Universe with whom you have a spiritual alliance. Those who forgot the alliance while in the throes of earth life, must actively and intentionally reinstate it. That is what you, as masters of greatness, are doing. You are remembering your truth that you brought with you into earth life.

Now then, the partnership has been discussed, the truth remembered, the alliance fully instated. The master of greatness now steps forth into his or her world with the assurance of great teamwork. Whatever now offers itself to your attention may be met with truth. The reservoir is there. The Partner is there. The decisions of how to enact truth will be teamed up between you, for you no longer work or live alone.

Yes, we now address you as masters, not candidates, for when you have fully entered into the partnership, when you have enacted the truth of your being by performing the deeds of masters, you ARE masters. Many of you will now try to wrest some particular meaning from what is said here. You may try to analyze the words, and the entering truth may seem too much too soon. You know your imperfections, your inadequacies! You think we may be premature in naming you masters. Not so. The partnership seals the bond, seals the way you will work. The entering truth now enacts because you depend on your Partner, and not upon yourself.

Even if you do feel that there is no entering greatness in your life, concentrate on the partnership. Even if you do not feel filled with power, do not hesitate to know you can use the Partner's power. That is what a partnership is — to provide the energy and the power to your thoughts. These thoughts generate themselves into focus as positive needs to be met or as desires that must be honored. Turn to the partnership, not to your own wavering which is only the passing thrust of earth truth trying to wrest you back into its message.

Give greatness its test, Masters of Greatness! The time for graduation is approaching!

Now put on the mantle of your master's degree. The earth plane offers its master degrees and the recipients receive paper while they wear the colorful mantles. That is their symbol, the colorful mantle. That you may enter into this new degree that spirit offers, we urge you to wear the mantle that we now describe.

This mantle eternalizes the wearer as one with God, the one in the partnership who will enter into the New Age to put the wonderful truth into action. The wearer of the mantle is the one whom we now enter into our rolls as the perfect trusted leader who will instate truth into the earth plane. The mantle that we propose here is invisible to earth eyes, but it is very visible to those who see with the eyes of spirit. This mantle eternalizes each wearer and teams him or her up with greatness manifested.

The mantle that is seen with the eyes of spirit has many colorful designs on it, designs that have deep meaning for the wearer and for the viewer. One design is of the gem you call a diamond. This gem shines and reflects the perfect Light of the Universe — the one God who brings forth all that is true and good. This gem is repeated in the pattern of your mantle ten times, each time representing the ten eternalizations that offer themselves as reminders of all that you can now accomplish.

These are (1) offering God power to protect people from the earth changes that devastate the entire surface of the earth; (2) providing that which supplements whatever truth people now have with God truth; (3) pouring out the way to glorious happiness because there is God truth to bring help to all mankind; (4) offering hope to people that they too can team up with God in the way you have teamed up; (5) making eternalizations of good for each person who asks; (6) opening yourself to the needs of others; (7) showing the ways of God that manifest in the New Age to bring new happiness and new goodness; (8) opening minds wherever you speak or appear; (9) offering those who do not want help your tender appreciation to let them go their ways in peace, and (10) not judging those who try and think they have failed to receive peterstet truth;

then providing them the means, through your own spirit, of attaining that truth.

The eternalizations listed above mean that you enter into earth activities as named when you and your Partner choose. The partnership is within the entity who wears the mantle, and the mantle is his reminder of what the true partnership will accomplish. Therefore, see with the eyes of spirit the diamonds that remind you of the ten eternalizations.

The other design on the mantle is woven in the fabric with gold thread. This design is of pure gold, that which will not be corrupted nor exploited. The design is the reminder to the wearer that there is no teamwork accomplished alone. That which is incorruptible is God. That which does not exploit for purposes of personal power is, of course, your Partner. Therefore, this design is your name, your spirit name that is chosen by you and your teacher.

The writer's design is "Truth-giver," and it is written in the language that gentle spirits know and produce. The name, not put into English, is, however, the same in meaning. The design reaches forth from the mantle to imprint itself on the mind of this writer.

So it is with the other masters of greatness. The design will interlock with the ten diamonds to make a personalized mantle. The overall mantle is partly white, partly green, the green of the trees that hold their heads high in the upper reaches of the earth. The mantle will have no heavy weight, for masters of greatness are not to feel any weight from their new eternalization. The white of great purity and the green of the tree tops combine with the perfect opulent thread that outlines the diamonds.

Now do you see the mantle? Now do you hold your shoulders proudly erect in order to wear the mantle designed to eternalize your perfect partnership?

Now receive your mantle, Master of Greatness!

That which is conferred upon you today is not given lightly or without much eternalizing on our part. We hold the mantle forth only to those who go the entire route, the entire walk with the textbook leading the way. The ones who stand here today to receive this mantle enter into the perfect Brotherhood of God.

The writer stands there amazed! This one did not understand that we are masters, that we have been training new masters in order to meet the requirements of the New Age. But yes, it is true. We in the Brotherhood of God have no thought of selfishness to give this venture. We only want to open the truth to those who, in earth form, must meet the inevitable teamwork required in the New Age.

* * * *

Those who now go forth with mantles upon their shoulders need to know their responsibilities, their opportunities, their obligations as masters. The first of these responsibilities is given to you by the Brother we call the One Who Brings Greatness.

Responsibilities of masters of greatness

Be open to my words, my thoughts, my purest intentions. To be a master of greatness, you who have today received the mantle must remember three responsibilities. The greatest one of these is the responsibility to the partnership itself. The master who puts ego before the partnership is entering into trouble because the power runs out quickly when we try to enter truth by our own power. The power source is the Partner, not the ego, remember. Therefore, to humble the Partner and to elevate the ego is entering your whole mission into destructiveness.

There is only one responsibility that you may never neglect and that is the one to the perfect partnership between you and the God of the Universe. Therefore, the stress must be put upon this one understanding.

Eternalizations of the entering truth will be successful only when the partnership is working fully; if the eternalizations seem not to work, it is because you have abandoned the partnership.

The second responsibility that is needed is to bring forth the truth, not the answer to needs. This means that the truth is to be instated, not the eternalization of a plant or other physical form. Instead, hold out the generosity of God, the perfection that produces all that anyone needs. Hold up the truth for all to see. Then hold up the item that will result from this truth.

The third responsibility is that of your growing understanding that applies to your own being. Whatever you produce in the outer is the result of the partnership, not of your own being. But when you start receiving credit, you may start people believing in your own personal greatness instead of the potential greatness that is possible because of the partnership.

An analogy may be taken about how the bank produces interest on your investment. If you remove your money from the bank and tell everyone that you will now produce the interest, not only will there be no interest, there will be no one to believe you know anything. Therefore, keep invested in the idea that the power is not within you, or you may reap the rewards of nothingness.

The God of the Universe is that vast Presence, wonderful Truth,perfect Understanding and the proper Answer that people need and want. But to take yourself from this Source is to remove the powerful teamwork that will produce what must be produced in the New Age. You can be certain that God is not jealous, for God is more than man, is He not? You can be certain that God does not insist on taking credit, for God is Principle, Law, Entering Truth. Then why must you enter the entire process into God? Because God is the holder of the power, the gifts, the perfection that you must have. To turn from God is the same as turning from the bank that has interest to dispense.

Those who enter today into this Brotherhood are most welcome here. We who are your brothers will help you in every way to do what you must do to help the earth in its travail, to help people in their travails.

Therefore, know that the teamwork is in place and you may now move to use it.

* * * *

The next Brother will bring a message on the way you may use your new master of greatness confirmation. He is the Brother we call Peter, the Entering Truth.

The way to eternalize opportunities

The way you masters of greatness will team up with your opportunities is to wrest each truth that you want to work with into the earth expression. Your truth is now teamed up within you to express your partnership, not just the entity that you are in spirit. Graduation from student to master means you are now in a partnership, not operating as a single spirit/mind. Hold onto this understanding, as it is basic to what I now tell you.

Bring yourself and your Partner into our meeting place in the temple of your being where you work with truth. This place is where the partnership operates. You who were of small stature now rise to the dimensions of greatness and intertwine with the One Who brings you truth that must be instated into the earth.

Be open minded, open and prepared to bring forth whatever is ready to come forth. With each pair (partnership) the truth will be different. You already expected this, did you not? Then hold yourself still, and team up with your Partner here in the sanctuary of your being.

The writer wonders if a teacher will be required. No, that one is now entered into other business, for you are now placed where we always intended to place you — in partnership with the God of the Universe. Therefore, in order to open your mind, you only need to open in trust to the One Who enters to be one with you.

God is that which enters your being with what God IS! That which He IS will never lead you astray nor will it bring you disappointment. Team up! Here is the perfect opportunity to be whatever you want to be!

The Partner will enter into whatever you express and will bring forth the truth concerning it. The writer has entered two concerns here in the temple of her being. These concerns which team up with her Partner give forth their energy. The Partner expresses truth to her spirit self and she begins, then, to work with the truth, not the effect she wants to achieve.

Now is your opportunity to bring forth greatness because there is no impediment to whatever you have set as a goal. Your truth must proclaim itself by pushing into the outer substance exactly what the truth IS. Therefore, if you choose to eternalize better growth in your spirit self, hurl the truth into that which you eternalize. The Partner will express the truth behind the act.

The truth may be "That which responds to spirit must rise to its potential." Then you will put that truth into the earth situation. Give it your teamwork, and God will give it His. The growth will then reach its potential, for the truth is entered.

However, masters of greatness must work **with** their Partners, not with the thought of talking with the Brotherhood. The Brotherhood have been here always, even as they are now. But it is you and your Partner who will produce the eternalization, not you and the Brotherhood. Those in the Brotherhood meet you whenever you wish, but we talk spirit to spirit in the way that those who have the God truth within them like to share and to express themselves. But the One Who now works totally with you is that God expression known as your Partner.

Thousands upon thousands of masters now respond to what is written here. Think of this! There are thousands of you who have chosen the partnership that will provide the greatness that will manifest. The partnerships seem to the more casual observer to be fragmentations of God. But those who have entered into the partnership to learn from it, know that the

God of the Universe is not to be contained within the individual mind. Why not? Because God is more than we can hope to eternalize. Therefore, put aside any thoughts of trying to explain what or who God IS. Why wrestle with what is impossible to explain? Enter into acceptance of Him, that wonderful Goodness present in the universe and able to team up with you individually.

To be God's partner, you must recognize the opportunity, not pick the explanation to death because you do not have the capacity to understand it.

* * * *

The next teammate will address the subject of your obligations. These team up with the truth that goes forth into the earth plane, the truth you send to be the earth substance. The one who will bring this message is the one we call Teammate Who Knows Truth.

Obligations to put into your teamwork

Those who now eternalize the truth that the Partner brings into the situation, whatever it is, have the obligation to give truth generously to others. This obligation is entered into the very heartbeat of the God of the Universe. Generosity is basic to the eternalizations that express truth.

Therefore, the first obligation to put into your teamwork is that very generosity that God IS. Now work with this thought to wrest from it all that it must say to you. Go into the temple of your being with your Partner and examine this obligation together.

When you have discussed this with your Partner, team up with me again to hear the next obligation.

Bring your being eternal truth that it may not wander afar in its quest to serve humanity. Eternal truth is that collection of principles, laws and teamed up individual truth that guides each person in expressing God truth. The obligation here is to adhere to eternal truth in the outworking of your mission.

There will be some of you whose mission is to protect the wildlife in the earth plane. To do this, you must work with eternal truth regarding those animals in this way. Review the earth's rules — the ones involving the purity of the earth, for example. (Earth rules provide the earth with wisdom that comes to it through you from the God of the Universe.) Then when you work with those wild creatures, use the purity principles in reviving their habitat. Enter into no misunderstanding here. That eternalization to wrest wildlife into the New Age with vigorous health is teamed up with the good of the earth. But to accomplish it, work within the laws and the principles. You may need to use this series of tomes (books) to review this part.

Everyone whose assignment is to reinstate good truth into the earth plane in one way or another will need to use eternal truth to accomplish the aims. Otherwise, you will involve your partnership in a hit or miss operation that will take much time to unravel. The Partner, if consulted, will review eternal truth with you. But if you decide to leap without eternal truth, the results may vary from nothing to very little.

Team up now to learn another obligation — that of the mercies that God pours on all creation. That which you will accomplish must be teamed up with these mercies that are part of God, or else the teamwork will go amiss. We say in all of these obligations that God's nature must be taken into account or there will be no demonstration.

Give yourself over to this God nature, for to do otherwise is to block the flow of power. To open to demonstration and not be open to the truth that whatever demonstration you perform must be of God is to speak in contradictions. Be single minded. Be God centered. Be aware of these obligations to the perfection of truth instated in earth. Then your eternalization will not go amiss; it will become substance.

The next obligation reviews another open truth. It is the underlying reason for the teamwork — that you will not go forth filled with the idea of personal power or the thought of fame and fortune. That which you pour onto the earth must, of necessity, be open to God's expression, not just your own expression. In this way the truth will prosper the earth and the people without the ebbing of power that will destroy even as you try to create. To work against yourself would be tantamount to pouring oil upon the very water you want to produce for drinking. First comes the purity, but also there comes pollution. The obligation you now have is to hold yourself close to your Partner without taking credit and without building an empire.

The lessons that are implied in these obligations have seen their expensive truth demonstrated in times past. But people seldom learn from the mistakes of others. They tend to repeat the mistakes. But now is the time to express truth with boldness and without the selfish self interest that will destroy all that can be gained.

There is a point to be made for those of you who know your own past lifetime experiences. You may now realize why you must stand upon these obligations with a firmness of purpose unparalleled in history. Perhaps you have, in a past lifetime, poured out the power-hungry approach only to bring devastation upon others and eventually upon yourself. Those who know this eternal truth that now must be put into the earth probably understand only too well what I mean.

Give, and it will be given you. Hold onto your good and it will express for others or for you. Team up with the Partner and the process of demonstration will give the earth and people whatever is needed to make life beautiful. Go ahead without the Partner and you will be trying to accomplish good with your own blistered bare hands. Receive your Partner's greatness gently, and you will give much of value. Push and force the greatness through, and you only achieve poor understanding that will water the earth with discouragement.

Yours is the energy, the pouring out of goodness, the eternalizations of greatness.

This chapter now ends. Its length has been greater than any chapter we have ever given the writer. But, the subject is that which now eternalizes within the Brotherhood to pour forth to you new masters of greatness. You who have received your mantles today are entered on our rolls here in this next plane of life. You will receive special generosity on the part of our entire Brotherhood. Open your mind to know this brightness that now pours itself upon your being and which eternalizes you within the partnership of the God of the Universe.

The New Age Enters with Tender Teamwork

19

A year after "Masters of Greatness" was written, I reviewed it before sending it to our printer for publishing in book form. As I began to read Chapter 19, I received this message which I include as a preface to the rest of the chapter.

"Open My Being to the reader. Say, 'We are now one in energy, one in manifestation.'"

Teaming up with those who want to help you through the troubles and the trials of the New Age will make your work smooth, your energy steady. Those who want to be your aides will stand by you who are masters, those who can save the planet and its people from hopeless teamwork. We in the Brotherhood offer our good help, our steady presence, our best energy to support those of you who will take on much in the way of recovery.

The New Age will be teamed up with eternalizations of each person who survives. That you may not fall prey to those eternalizations that proclaim the end of the world, the holocaust, the terrible times eternalized within the Bible, we want to proclaim the way this New Age can be when you and other masters work in your partnerships.

The earth will indeed tremble with the great change that will take place. The times will signify to you that the best is now ready to present itself, not the worst. Trembling signifies only that the earth will turn on its side, respond to a new polar mark and then continue its orbit around the sun.

Because the earth will begin to change violently in some ways, but only gradually in others, people will tend to be frightened. They will foresee the end of the world. They will foresee God's punishment and fall to their knees in fear. They will turn to the eternalization of their deaths and stop trying to work or to help others. Yes, many will be immobilized.

But you who know the truth, and there are now many of you, will know that truth is ready to manifest. Those who are masters will take their places as leaders without waiting for an assignment from others. You will gather whatever number of people you can, and you will tell them that you knew this time would come, that it has been foretold, that it is merely the earth replenishing itself with purity, with truth that will help it to become perfect substance once again.

People may question you, but tell them this one thing and no more.

"I AM the one named to help people in this New Age. There are many more like me, and everyone who is to help and lead you will come forth to do so. The time is now when the truth we once held to be vitally important will no longer help us. Where are the computers? They have no power. Where are the many supplies, the stores, the suppliers? Where are the jobs we went to each day? Where are the houses, the buildings, all that we once eternalized as necessities of life? They are gone. Therefore, know that there are other answers, other truth that you must learn if you are to survive."

Most people will want leadership. Most will cry out to you to guide them. Then here is your plan, in essence, for we cannot tell you now exactly what to do. The reason we know you will operate with greatness is that you have the Partner who teams up with you and produces the powerful thoughts into substance.

This Partner is your Mainstay, your Source of Wisdom, your Powerful Ally, your Perfect Gentle Companion who will bring the leadership you proclaim into truth.

"But," you may say to yourself, "will I be able to perform like you say? Will I revert to my own earth-mind truth that will bring me to my knees in fear?"

You will not fail if you turn now to the God of the Universe — that which is your Partner — with your whole heart, your whole mind, your whole being.

Here is an example to illustrate what we say.

There is a master who lives now in India where he performs his greatness in a poor village called Eternal Truth (its spirit name). The one who enters with his Partner eternalizes this place as that which produces what it needs to feed the people. The climate is harsh; the summer is short; the energy of the sun cannot reach the plants to bring them to their maturity because the mountains hide the sun much of the day.

Yet the gardens flourish; the people know nothing of earth-mind truth which says these vegetables should not grow. They know nothing of the earth-mind truth that says fruit trees will not thrive in such an environment. Therefore, when the master says that they can grow whatever they need to feed themselves, they do it. Their gardens respond only to God, to the Partner which the master brings to each problem.

The people not only eat well, they eternalize the shelter they need in that mountainous area. The master points out to them that they need materials that will provide warmth, that will provide certain comforts, that will allow them refuge in harsh weather and will provide places where gatherings of people will study and learn how to use truth in glorious ways. There is nothing in the earth plane with which to compare these shelters.

These people live happy productive lives by whispering the truth to their own body selves. They know they are spirit; they know they can direct what is physical, what is the glorious truth of the universe. Their master is the earthly guide who generously lives his life as their servant, not their powerful leader. His life and work is the point of what we say here — that a master must be turned completely toward the Partner to be the effective guide that people will need.

The object of this chapter is to show you how masters work in the cluster of people whom they gather together. The master must be perfectly centered, not fragmented. Those people who wail and weep must be put aside to wail and weep together. Others must be brought round you while you paint the picture of what can happen in this cluster if all work together. Give them opportunities to pull apart from the group. Then hold those who stay to their bargain — that they will work with new truth that will bring them into a new and better life than they have ever known.

This promise is given by the God of the Universe, and those in the Brotherhood know it is true. We stand here in this plane to help in all ways, to bring our beings into any and all situations, to hold to the truth which will be demanded in this time of unrest.

I interrupted to ask, "What if a master finds himself or herself the only leader for a large number of people? What is the master whose speciality is shelter supposed to do when people are hungry?"

Those who know how to build shelter with God truth will be able to feed people too. The one who turns to his Partner to outline the needs and ask for help will find that help forthcoming. Therefore, if the speciality is then entered into evidence, those people will be ready to understand how their food supply enters, will they not?

I wasn't so sure. I could well imagine our environment changing, and I could understand people needing food and shelter. People would be in shock, frightened; some would be belligerent, perhaps. And there I would be, a master of greatness, one whose speciality is writing books! What kind of leadership could I give?

Those who have specialties must work with their Partners to arrive at the needed mastery in more than one area. This does not change your specialty, you understand, but it does mean that you must learn to operate truth in whatever circumstances you find yourself. The master we told you of who lives in India has as his specialty the great poetry of universal wisdom. But yet he can help those in that isolated village to live their lives with greatness. Why? Because he practices the universal truth that his Partner brings to him and which his Partner materializes within his being.

The words moved me, but I could not see me as such a master.

The being that you are — that purple, blue and pink spirit self — has the partnership of the greatest force there is in the universe! Why wonder at what is now given you — that Being's entering Presence, God'scollaboration on that which means greatness manifests?

After giving much thought to the above paragraph, I stopped writing in order to get my own answers, to settle my own questions. Impatience, my undoing in spiritual matters, had to question, to worry over the answers, to try to force manifestation. As usual, when I step forth with just my own ego, I fall on my face. Instead of truly accepting my Partner's words, I persisted in being uneasy, querulous and being the supreme doubter of my power as master.

Finally, my Partner addressed me in a way that got my full attention.

Truth — if shot out of a gun — would satisfy you! But because truth goes forth on soft feet, slipping quietly into all that awakens to it, you have no earth sense of its going forth!

Become quiet. Become My quiet partner who listens, but who does not talk. Quietly release your concerns to My Good. Watch truth unfold; watch its power center on each project (we have). Move mountains with greatness, not with your earth tools of haste and opinions.

One day I'll write a book about our projects — my Partner's and mine. Then I can explain what they are and how good develops when I take my hands off and let Pure Power work them through.

My Partner continued.

The perfection that each master wants will happen if that master does not outline the perfection himself. That perfection is the potential possible in situations, in objects, in whatever the master sees that needs attention.

When the master points to a child who needs the understanding of wholeness, he may see only the broken leg or the withered hand. But My Power sees the potential and calls it forth. The child who is lame will walk, but he will not be the same child who lay on the ground awaiting wholeness. No! He will rise with new truth within him, new understanding ready to be put into the earth plane. That is the perfection that individuals, even masters, may not see. But when they are one with their Teammates, the One who enters to give power to truth, then the potential is realized in each and every situation.

The Brotherhood again addressed the new masters.

Now rise in thought to that which we now point out to you, new masters of greatness. That which the God of the Universe ordains is now ordained to become one in purpose, one in eternal truth and one in the total and absolute God potential. Therefore, you who use this teamwork to help earth and its people will find that same truth working with you. You who may feel weak will overcome weakness because that which you begin to use now will bring your own potential into view. You will not be the same woman or man who now accepts this ordination. You will no longer be the hesitant individual who hopes to be worthy. You will be the manifestation of greatness, the perfection that your being calls forth — your potential!

Therefore, think not to go along from this point onward as the hesitant, hopeful person who wants to be God's worthy partner. It will develop in this way. You will find yourself at the heights of understanding, the heights of open truth that pours into your mind throughout the hours of the day. That which you are, the pure self, the pure being, will manifest what is your destiny to manifest — your oneness with God.

Rise to meet your opportunities now. Do not wait for the New Age. Go to work now, at this very moment. That which presents itself to you as a need in the earth plane, no matter what that need is, hold it up to the powerful light of your Partner, and then team up with that Partner to bring goodness into manifestation.

The writer wonders if anyone is already working in the manner we outline. There are many who already work in this way, many masters who now understand their role in the partnership. These who have this understanding open their minds to the greatness, and with quiet understanding, let their Partners bring forth whatever is the potential in the given concern.

One master, a woman who wants to work totally in the partnership, teamed up with whatever was her own potential. She entered into meditation daily, held out her thoughts to others, and then she held various concerns in her mind. These concerns went out to her Partner who held them in His own hands, in His own Being, in His own thrust of power. These concerns quietly, without fanfare, went back to those whose understanding was less than pure, and their concerns received their perfect answers. This master enters life full of awareness — awareness of what mankind is needing, is seeking, is ready for. Then she raises the concern to her Partner with the assurance of His perfect answer.

Though what we say here sounds somewhat like conventional prayer, there is a great deal of difference. Those who want to help others must do so in spirit, in the total uplifting of an individual or a concern. To hold up a lame person as one who walks is not the full potential, masters of greatness. The full potential is that core of each person, that spirit self who gives the body its orders. That spirituality is what we work with.

Put aside your ideas of making the sick well just to be well. There is much more to your work than this.

The spirit must be addressed to become its potential. Now go forth with this in mind, and work with your Partner that you will be ready when the New Age catches you unexpectedly. When that time arrives, you will need to work night and day to bring forth the potential in many, many situations and in many, many people who will not know what you speak of.

This entering of truth is now coming to a close. We team up with you in our perfect understanding to help you receive perfect understanding. We who stand here in this next plane of life understand your eternal problems, but we will remind you that you can now act with authority, with the reasonableness that a master of greatness will come to expect.

The Most Helpful Person in the New Age

20

The final chapter of this book is full of challenges and reassurances for new masters of greatness. No matter how difficult the work of the New Age will be and how lonely the path of the masters, the goals are certain to be reached, according to those who help to bring these books to you.

The eternal truth will manifest in the New Age because you, masters of greatness, know how to apply truth to the new conditions of earth. There will be much wrong thinking when the earth reaches its new polarity, but you will hold firmly to the truth which will enter your mind through your personal God-mind connection, through the partnership that you have formed.

No pursuing doubt will overtake you because you are teamed up with the Partner who will enter into your work in an intimate way. Your teamwork will be that of ONE, not two separate entities. There will never be just you — the egocentric individual — who turns his mind to helping people. The master refers to the entity who is teamed up perfectly with the Pure Truth, with the Teammate or Partner who becomes ONE in mind, ONE in purpose, ONE is design.

When the partnership is used in this way, nothing stands in the way of accomplishment. That which is

God is within you, and that which is the individual entity — you — is teamed up within that perfect Partner. Where does one begin and the other leave off? Entering truth will not indicate the individual nor the Partner, for you (the partnership) will operate as ONE. Therefore, when you enact the truth, you will be acting within the partnership.

Be assured that what we say is very true, that you have turned in your individualities in favor of partnerships. Be entirely without awe and without cautiousness, for you (the partnerships) are eternal truth centers — eternal bright centers of hope and extreme optimism. Now pay attention! When we say "you," we mean the partnership, not the individual who entered into this study. There is no use for an individual in the New Age, but there is much use for partnerships. When you think of yourself in relationship to the world around you, think "we." That is the needed element that will hold you to your task.

Your mantle hangs well over your shoulders. The Brothers here who want only to help you in your work wear their mantles too. We — you, the master, and we, the Brothers — are all One in God, One in Truth, One in Commitment. We end any allegiance to what we once held to be great earth truth because we know that earth truth will not suffice. We must hold only to God truth here, only to the eternalizations that we, within our partnerships, can hold forth to bring earth and its people into the New Age with great assurances.

Whatever the teamwork, whatever the open truth, you will be the ones to bring greatness into manifestation in the New Age. This chapter is devoted to that time and that work and to you, masters of greatness, who will be the most helpful persons in the New Age.

Yours is the mission, yours is the assignment, yours is the great hope for greatness manifested. The partnerships are in place around the globe. Yours is one of many thousands of partnerships developed to meet the New Age. Therefore, when you work, work with the certainty that others, like you and your Partner, are working in similar fashion. The masters stand forth in partnership to teach others how to depend upon God truth, how to enter into the alliance with this greatness, how to form the partnerships. You will not work on your own for long, should that be the case, for you will soon have more masters to aid in this heavy work load.

The reflection we want to add to this book concerns the opening of the New Age to turmoil. The truth is that the turmoil is going into the earth plane even as this book is being written. This means by the time the book is in the marketplace, the turmoil will be clearly visible. We who have been watching the signs now want to assure you that everything is as foretold within our books. The earth is heaving its gasps, its entering travail, its new eternalization that calls for new purity. We in this plane see it all clearly, but yet we do not want to enter into negative thoughts concerning the planet. We want to help to ameliorate the situation so that the earth will not belch forth its eternalization to the destruction of mankind! We try to hold the earth in our clear sight of gradually turning to its new polarity. When you read this, team up with our thoughts in the matter that we will, together, ease the turmoil.

Every person who wants the earth to survive must hold to the picture of caring for the earth. Each thought, each act of caring will help to bring the earth into line with our thoughts of easing the turmoil. If uncaring thoughts go forth, if selfishness persists, the earth may need to belch forth its eternalization to get past the barriers the energy of earth truth sets up. Therefore, team up with us now to hold the powerful thought form that the earth is welcome to provide for its new purity, that there is no opposition, no sense of terrible destruction, only thoughts of cooperation! Then we help this material earth to respond to its spiritual center which, in turn, responds to our thought projection of goodness instated within the earth.

You, new masters of greatness, now enter the New Age with the certainty of your own partnerships —

with the Pure Truth which rises within you, with the powerful thrust of energy that stands back of Pure Truth — to bring greatness into manifestation. This is our core message. You are now ready to graduate even past your present point into post graduate study. This study will take you into the far reaches of the universe to practice whatever you must in order to perform your tasks in the New Age.

To receive post graduate studies, you must read the third book in the trilogy, **Truth for the New Age.** This book, titled "The Eternal Teamwork," is the third book in the series. It outlines your teamwork profiles and the way your partnerships will generate power to bring truth into action. It will also give a profile of how the New Age may appear to those on earth. A discussion of the perfection that both you and the world receive when Pure Truth is used is included in this book. Assignments will be pressed into forms that you can understand, and the New Age will be entered into the viewbook that you may see for yourself, in advance, how the world will appear. That way you will not be surprised, nor will you be hopeless or discouraged by the earth itself. The viewbook is only to set your thinking upon what the planet must rest — Pure Truth. Remember, earth-mind truth will not be of use.

You will be required to use a generous amount of your time to pursue work that even now must be done to ready yourself for the New Age. Then humble thoughts will eliminate themselves in favor of more powerful greatness. Humble thoughts have no place in the New Age. You will need to use great thoughts.

The new book also will hold before you patterns of thought that might be useful to you in bringing truth into focus and into the manifested substance. There will be applications of truth presented that may help you to work easily as you begin this serious activity. There will be a power distribution to each partnership that will bring with it great purpose and results. The energizing is that which is of God, not of us!

Wear your mantles with pride, for though they are newly arranged upon your shoulders, they signify the mighty partnership that will save those who enter the New Age. Wear them with the eternalization of the partnership, the entering awareness of the diamonds and the symbol of your own spirit name. This design holds you to the remembrance of the commitment you have entered into, of the perfect partnership that is now resting upon your shoulders.

You whom we now address have the greatness within your grasp, within your spirit that blends with your Partner's Greatness. The next book will end the series of tomes that were assigned to this writer. This entity may then be free to cultivate whatever she wishes to cultivate in the way of writing or in any activity she wishes to enter into. This present tome will mark the conclusion of that long ago commitment made by her to enter life to perform the tasks assigned.

We who stand with the writer in bringing this material from the heart of the God of the Universe know that each book has remarkable impact upon the world. To wrest this power into your bright, energetic lifetimes, you only have to hold your mantle upon your shoulders. Whether you now work for others, for the planet or for your own personal circumstance, it is all the same with your Partner. Therefore, take all concerns, not just universal ones, to this One. Be totally open to your Partner who will initiate His power into your life experience. Team up with the thought that you will not be thinking of any duality of your own being. You who are now masters, who are now living your lifetimes, can team up to bring greatness into all aspects of life — your personal lives, the entire planet and the needs and requirements of others.

Partners are one in all things, not just in certain ones. Hold no concern as unworthy of your Partner's attention. To live your life in close association, you must hold out the totality of your life experience and the totality of your observations and your entire thought plan that operates within. The partnerships have the generous power of the bright Goodness that God IS. Use this power.

Make no alliance with any individual who is not entered into truth. To identify yourself too closely with one who does not enter into the understanding that is now within you, is to turn your face away from the brightness of God. Yes, the teamwork is either singly identified or it is not identified at all. Hold yourself within the partnership, but make no outcry to others that you need their approval or their opinions on the matter. You and your Partner are now identified as ONE, and there is no room in this partnership for a third party. The partnerships may abound, but they all have one entity plus the Partner.

Reason and truth must prevail together, not reason without truth. Preachers may appeal to your reason, saying, "We in the church have the understanding that we have had through the years. Heed our explanation for this new turn of events!" Their appeal to reason is not teamed up with truth. Their ideas have not generated power, nor have they generated teamwork between man and God. Therefore, their appeals to reason are their own brands of earth truth, not the combination that works — reason and truth.

The Brothers in this second plane of life have said they will help you, but yet you may wonder just how, since the partnerships are what matter. But we who know the way of truth and who realize the need you may have of help, will be present with our own partnerships to sustain you no matter how hard the task, how tiring the ordeals, how worrisome the needs. We will go forth as emissaries to those who need help, to you if you need help, to bring our own best efforts to the spiritual core of individuals, to situations, to whatever causes you alarm or concern.

We here in this plane will not let you work alone, even if you find no other master in the earth plane. We will be there to energize your body, to hold your bodily self upright and strong, to keep you single minded and pure in thought. We will not let you weaken, even if you sometimes want to weaken. The Brothers here have their own mantles, their own partnerships, their own helpful methods of assisting. Simply think of the help you need and let us team up with you. There will be such a feeling within you of great eternal truth that is coming forth, that you will be restored to strength and to optimistic undertaking of this very difficult job of being a master of greatness.

Teaming up with the plan that now brings you into the New Age, you are ready to take on the responsibilities, the opportunities and the obligations of a full master. We who assist you in whatever way possible, now give you this thought — you now reside within the Oneness of God. This means, of course, that you now open your mind, even as other great entities opened their beings, to the planet upon which you live and to the people who live thereon. You are the ONE in ONE who enters the New Age with the Pure Truth that will bring new hope, new truth, new eternalizations. Be what you must be and be it in totality, for yours is the perfection, the entering goodness, the eternal power of the universe.

Those who have gone before stand here in this plane, surrounding you who turn your face toward us, to remind you of your destiny. Enter now with the certain eternalization of you as the One in One, for that is what you are!

GLOSSARY

advanced souls — All souls (spirit entities) come to planet earth with growth plans. Those who enact these plans in their earth lives are referred to as "advanced."

agape love — There are many kinds of love. Agape refers to love that helps one another, not a love that encompasses a person with affection.

automatic writing — This kind of writing is a process the writer uses to record the mind to mind communication between her and the Brotherhood of God. It ties into the writer's inner perception of thoughts that pour into her open mind through the open channel.

Bible — A collection of stories, history and remembrances that gives the progression of thought about God. It is a guide for living, divinely inspired, but it is not the only word of God. The word of God comes to each individual as a flow of wisdom, and the Bible — at best — is but one source of wisdom. God — a living, pulsating, vibrant energy — is the Source of Pure Truth, not a Bible — any Bible.

Brotherhood of God — Advanced spirits stay nearby in the next plane of life to enact the work of the Holy Spirit. They are the counselor, the comforter, the teacher who work with those in the earth plane who open their minds to them. These spirits are helpers who want to help people team up with the God of the Universe to receive eternal and personal truth.

channel — An individual who is called a channel is only proving that there is communication possible between those in the earth plane and those in the next plane of life. Anyone can be a channel through which the Mind of God pours individual and eternal truth.

channelled writing — When mind to mind communication is written, it is often called channelled writing. However, all inspired writing — be it poetry, stories, essays, even music or artistic expression is to be considered channelled.

christ — This is a concept of oneness with God. Each person can consider himself or herself the Christ in the sense of that oneness. When we acknowledge the Christ, we acknowledge our oneness with God.

claim — Your way of calling to the powerful forces of God.

devil — Here is a concept many people hold in mind to explain what they call "evil." This concept of an evil presence within a person diminishes the concept of God by keeping the individual focused on the absence of what God IS.

demonstration — Basically, demonstration is the process of producing your thought into the physical world. The success of the process is predicated upon a person's understanding and application of spiritual principles.

earth-bound spirits — When souls — or spirits — separate from their bodies and live in the next plane of life, some cannot let go of their earth life identities. These spirits are called "earth-bound."

earth-mind — Earth-mind goes no further than man has gone. It proves its beliefs in material substance, historical data, scientific observations. Earth-mind also embraces religion as a worthy effort to reach God. But God is often demoted to that which holds society together in values, not a personal entity Whose vastness is yet to be proved in individual lives.

energy — Enate power that rises from your truth — either God-mind or earth-mind.

entity — When an individual is called an "entity," the reference is to the inner being or spirit self.

emptying (yourself) — This is a process of clearing the mind of tempermental thoughts and personal ego in order to receive God's truth. Meditation, willingness to let go of personal beliefs, and trusting your highest concept of God are examples of emptying.

eternalization — This term refers to the goal or object you visualize along with the helpers from the Brotherhood. They and you work with your God truth to visualize what is needed, what is wanted. Then, the three in one — the Holy Spirit, the spirit of the individual and the power of the God of the Universe produce any generous and worthy thought into earth substance. Also, see ***mold.***

gentle or tender presences — These spirits work within the Brotherhood/Holy Spirit to reunite your being with God spirit. With the help of these presences, those in the earth plane can meet every need or concern with positive, perfect understanding. With their help, each person can be useful in his society and can help meet the needs of others as well as himself.

God-force — This term refers to the power of God that acts according to truth principles. This power manifests thoughts into things.

God the Father, God the Judgment, etc. — Terms which indicate the extent of the concept people have about God. Words that follow "God" indicate what it is that people believe.

God of the Universe — This designation is meant to open your concept of God to the furthest reaches of your mind. The God concept must be expanded if it is to meet your best expectations. The smaller the God concept, the smaller the expectations; therefore, the Brotherhood tries to help each individual to open his/her mind to all that God Is.

God-mind — The unrestricted and unlimited Mind that produces a flow of wisdom that anyone can tap into is called God-mind. This truth that flows with a steady impulse wants to connect with the individual mind/spirits who reach out to become one with the God of the Universe. In this text the God-mind truth is called "peterstet" — that which satisfies perfectly, that which never runs out of energy.

God-mind truth — See ***God-mind.***

God-self — The entity or person who is teamed up with God.

God's emissary — A person who lives the truth of God.

growth — When a person accepts truth and lives it, spiritual growth occurs. This growth is that which becomes a permanent part of the spirit self.

growth plan — Before a soul or spirit enters an infant body within the womb, that entity made a plan to achieve oneness with God. This plan, if it was true to the nature of what is God, was a cooperative venture between the God of the Universe and the individual.

Holy Spirit — The Counselor, Comforter, Teacher which is the activity of the Holy Spirit is centered in those advanced spirits called the Brotherhood of God.

inner self — The reality of each person is the inner self or spirit/soul. This inner self has lived many lifetimes and will never die.

inner temple — To help us in our spiritual growth, it is recommended by the Brotherhood that we create within us an inner temple. This temple is a meeting place for our partnerships to receive Pure Truth, to study, meditate, learn.

Jesus — The Brother of Brothers (Jesus) became the outward manifestation of the inner being who lived his life according to his growth plan. Jesus the man reflected his inner self who enacted his oneness with God.

love — This term cannot be understood in human terms, for experience gives us erroneous ideas about love. Tenderness is the ultimate spiritual expression of total support and caring. Love is a servant of tenderness and bows before the ultimate expression because "love" gives and receives. Tenderness only gives.

manifestation — See ***demonstration.***

mind/spirit — The mind is separate from the brain. The brain is physical — material; the mind is spiritual. When the term "mind/spirit" is used, it refers to the reality within us — the soul or spirit which is capable, under any and all conditions, of connecting to all that God Is.

mold — An eternalization that a person holds in mind produces a mold for whatever you want to create in the earth plane.

New Age — The time now appears on the horizon when the earth must reinstate purity into its being. When this time comes, nothing will be as it was. Those who heed the truth of God, however, will help both planet and mankind to survive, to flourish and to live in total teamwork.

next plane of life — The earth plane is where our spirit selves — our souls — express in human form. The next plane of life interpenetrates the earth plane, and it is here that the Brotherhood of God work as the outreach of the Holy Spirit. It is also a place of coming and going — spirits leaving the earth plane and spirits preparing to re-enter life on planet earth.

open channel — The means by which the Brotherhood of God works with each individual to help bring about the God-mind connection.

partnership — The perfect oneness with God constitutes a true partnership. When masters of greatness enter freely into this oneness, they live as one with God.

peterstet truth — Personal and eternal truth from the Mind of God to the individual mind is called "peterstet" because it satisfies and enlightens each mind/spirit who receives it and uses it.

pontification — That which is thought, spoken or written in regard to spiritual matters.

prayer — Religionists practice prayer to bring mankind into mental attunement to their God concepts. Prayer offers hope, consideration and an opportunity for reverance. Prayer is seldom thought of as communication between God and man. It is usually a ritual connecting man to a God he cannot hope to understand.

reincarnation — Living one lifetime after another as men and women, as various nationalities, as members of all races, we have an opportunity to enact our growth plan and enact our oneness with God. Reincarnation is God's plan which gives people many opportunities for spiritual growth.

religion — An organization which brings people together in churches for the purpose of worship and to turn them into good workers. Generally, religion keeps people from their individual discovery of God.

replenishment — When people draw upon the gifts of God, when they respond to God truth, they replenish the earth and their lives with what is the nature of God.

Satan — Satan and the devil are not the same. Satan is the Old Testament personality who gives the personification of evil in many fictional stories. But Satan did not tempt people. He was the questioner who asked questions that people needed to answer and to understand their relationship with God.

spiritual law — Any God truth that operates within the universe as law — as that which must come about.

soul — See ***inner self.***

teamwork — This term is the basic strength of the work of spirit, for without the teamwork of the Brotherhood/Holy Spirit and the God of the Universe, there can be no accomplishment of permanent value. Teamwork takes each one who understands its strength into the realm of the masters who can bring earth materiality from the seed of God truth. ***Team up*** is the directive to join with the God of the Universe and the Brotherhood of God.

templing — By bringing God truth together with the inner spirit, the two are templed, or perfectly joined.

tenderness — See ***love.***

tension — Tension, tone and vibration are interconnected. Each person determines his spiritual tension or outreach for what is God; tension determines the spiritual tone which, in turn, affects the vibration of the spirit which probes for the flow of wisdom from God-mind.

teteract truth — This earth-mind truth encourages mankind toward his potential, but then this truth lets people down, for it does not have an extended, far-reaching and ultimate goodness within it.

thought-form — The human body is a thought-form, for it is the manifestation of that creative goodness which emanates through God. Other thought-forms are the manifested thoughts that we, with the help of the God of the Universe, bring into being.

tome — One book of a series of books which contain the truth that God has to impart.

tone — See ***tension.***

truth — Anything you believe in is your own truth. Truth, as you take it within and work with it, develops the fabric of your lifetime experience. Your truth consists of powerful thoughts that become the center or focus of your mind/spirit.

vibrations — See ***tension.***

wetness — When the Brotherhood of God uses the word "wetness" or "wet," the words denote discouragement in its various forms. "Wet truth" is earth-mind truth that leaves an individual without hope. "Wetness" is the quality of inferior truth that never comes from the Mind of God.

Jean Foster is an important writer, a very clear channel and one of the many who urge people to open their minds to new understanding of that vast goodness called God. Jean Foster's first three books, *The God-Mind Connection, The Truth That Goes Unclaimed,* and *Eternal Gold,* reveal the tenderness and wisdom of inner truth that pours from the God of the Universe into individuals. Her fourth book, *Epilogue,* confirms the principles revealed in this trilogy. These books have an enthusiastic following.

Masters of Greatness is the second book of her latest trilogy, **Truth for the New Age,** a three-part textbook to develop leadership who will help people make a successful passage through the earth changes. The first book of this trilogy, *New Earth — New Truth,* was published in 1989. The third book of this trilogy, *The Eternal Teamwork,* will be published in 1991.

TeamUp was specifically formed as a publishing company for producing and distributing all of the information which is being revealed through Jean Foster. This information is contributing to a worldwide awareness of God and mankind in a divine partnership that meets all needs and goals.

Readers interested in receiving periodic news bulletins concerning these books and other information which has been revealed through Jean Foster are encouraged to write directly to her. She is also interested in hearing from readers who have successfully applied the principles revealed in these books in their daily lives. Contact Jean Foster through:

TeamUp
Box 1115
Warrensburg, MO 64093

Also by Jean K. Foster

*The God-Mind Connection**

An account of the writer's communication with spirit counselors called The Brotherhood, this book provides instructions on finding and making your own personal God-mind connection. The first volume of a powerful trilogy, Jean Foster's book offers clear information on how to discover your true purpose and destiny.

141 pages, perfect bound, $8.95

*Also available on audio cassette. Album of six cassettes (5 1/2 hours of narration by Jean Foster), $34.95.

The Truth that Goes Unclaimed

In this second book in the *Trilogy of Truth,* after "The God-Mind Connection," Foster explores in detail the specific steps the reader may take to establish his personal God-mind connection and allow it to be a powerful force in his own life: how to clarify goals, form a greater God-image, build an Inner Temple, and experience truth in practical ways.

174 pages, perfect bound, $8.95

Eternal Gold

In a trilogy that helps readers claim the perfect truth available to each of them in everyday life, this final book of the *Trilogy of Truth* reaches forward into powerful new concepts and methods for enhancing life in every respect. Here the reader is shown how to deal directly with God and thus to address problems of health and prosperity as well as individual issues. Eternal gold is the God truth each one may claim, making life truly richer and more blessed.

143 pages, perfect bound, $8.95

Epilogue

What happens to us when we die? Where do we go? Will God punish us for our wrongdoings? Will we see Jesus? What will life be like in heaven? Will I join my parents or my spouse?

All of these questions and many more are answered in the fascinating stories told by departed spirits of what happens when we die and leave the earth plane.

According to the spirit entities contacted by the writer, the next plane of life is similar to the earth plane with some major exceptions. The greatest surprise, they say, is that "here everyone communicates by thought. They create by thought, and they even get what they need and desire by way of thought. If you want a stand of redwood trees in your backyard, that's what you get."

173 pages, perfect bound, $9.95

New Earth — New Truth

"New Earth — New Truth" is the first of three books in the trilogy *Truth for the New Age* which have been revealed to Jean Foster by the Brotherhood of God. These advanced spirits on another plane reveal — in an astonishing and candid manner — that the New Age is upon us. As an outreach of the Holy Spirit, the Brotherhood awakens the reader to the necessity of putting God-mind truth to work now, not waiting for the time of travail. Reassurances dominate this book, however, not pictures of gloom and doom.

195 pages, perfect bound, $9.95